First World War
and Army of Occupation
War Diary
France, Belgium and Germany

19 DIVISION
57 Infantry Brigade
Prince of Wales's (North Staffordshire Regiment)
8th Battalion
1 June 1915 - 31 January 1918

WO95/2085/2

The Naval & Military Press Ltd
www.nmarchive.com
Published in association with The National Archives

Published by

The Naval & Military Press Ltd

Unit 10 Ridgewood Industrial Park,

Uckfield, East Sussex,

TN22 5QE England

Tel: +44 (0) 1825 749494

www.naval-military-press.com

www.nmarchive.com

This diary has been reprinted in facsimile from the original. Any imperfections are inevitably reproduced and the quality may fall short of modern type and cartographic standards.

© **Crown Copyright**
Images reproduced by permission of The National Archives, London, England, 2015.

Contents

Document type	Place/Title	Date From	Date To
Heading	WO95/2085/2		
Heading	8th Bn Nth Staffs. Jly 1915-Jan 1918		
Heading	8 Batt The North Staffordshire Regiment. July (17.7.15-31.7.15) 1915		
War Diary	Southampton	17/07/1915	17/07/1915
War Diary	Havre	18/07/1915	18/07/1915
War Diary	Andrieq	21/07/1915	21/07/1915
War Diary	Nortbecourt	23/07/1915	23/07/1915
War Diary	Renescure	24/07/1915	24/07/1915
War Diary	Molinghem	25/07/1915	30/07/1915
War Diary	Merville	31/07/1915	31/07/1915
Heading	8th Battn The North Staffordshire Regiment. August (2.8.15-29.8.15) 1915		
War Diary	Near Merville	02/08/1915	02/08/1915
War Diary	Estaires	04/08/1915	04/08/1915
War Diary	Trenches	12/08/1915	19/08/1915
War Diary	Merville	21/08/1915	27/08/1915
War Diary	Paradis	28/08/1915	28/08/1915
War Diary	Trenches	29/08/1915	29/08/1915
Heading	8th Battn The North Staffordshire Regiment. September (2.9.15-29.9.15) 1915		
War Diary	Trenches	02/09/1915	13/09/1915
War Diary	Locon	21/09/1915	27/09/1915
War Diary	Le Hamel	29/09/1915	29/09/1915
Miscellaneous	Appendices I & II		
Miscellaneous Diagram etc	57th Brigade		
Heading	8th Batt The North Staffordshire Regiment. October (29.9.15-1.11.15) 1915		
War Diary	Trenches	29/09/1915	15/10/1915
War Diary	Lacoufore	16/10/1915	20/10/1915
War Diary	Trenches Ind 1b Sub-sector	20/10/1915	20/10/1915
Heading	8th Battn The North Staffordshire Regiment. November (5.11.15-25.11.15) 1915		
War Diary	Le Hamel	05/11/1915	05/11/1915
War Diary	Locon	10/11/1915	13/11/1915
War Diary	Rue Du Bois	17/11/1915	17/11/1915
War Diary	Trenches	21/11/1915	24/11/1915
War Diary	Locon	25/11/1915	25/11/1915
Heading	8th Battn The North Staffordshire Regiment. December (29.11.15-31.12.15) 1915		
War Diary	Robecq	29/11/1915	04/12/1915
War Diary	Cix Marmuse	05/12/1915	11/12/1915
War Diary	King's Road	15/12/1915	27/12/1915
War Diary	Le Toret	31/12/1915	31/12/1915
Heading	8th H. Stafford Vol 7 Jan 16		
War Diary	Le Touret	04/01/1916	04/01/1916
War Diary	Croix-Barbee	08/01/1916	24/01/1916
War Diary	Robecq	24/01/1916	31/01/1916
Miscellaneous	57th Brigade.	24/01/1916	24/01/1916

Type	Description	From	To
Heading	8 N Staffs Vol 9		
War Diary	Robecq	01/02/1916	19/02/1916
War Diary	Merville	24/02/1916	24/02/1916
War Diary	Riez Bailleul	26/02/1916	07/03/1916
War Diary	La Gorgue	15/03/1916	15/03/1916
War Diary	Reis Bailleul	16/03/1916	20/03/1916
War Diary	Chapigny Sector	21/03/1916	01/04/1916
Operation(al) Order(s)	Operation Order No 24	20/03/1916	20/03/1916
Miscellaneous	Special Order Of The Day by Major-General T. Bridges, C.M.G., D.S.O., Commanding 19th Division.	23/03/1916	23/03/1916
Miscellaneous	19th Division	23/03/1916	23/03/1916
Miscellaneous	Instruction And Information Re Minor Operations To Be Carried Out Night Of 20/21st March.		
Miscellaneous	Scheme For An Offensive Operation To Be Carried Out On 20/3/16	20/03/1916	20/03/1916
Miscellaneous	App A	20/03/1916	20/03/1916
Miscellaneous	Special Order of the Day by Major-General T. Bridges, C.M.G. D.S.O. Commanding 19th Division.	29/03/1916	29/03/1916
Miscellaneous	Action Of Trench Mortar Batteries For Night 20th/21st March 1916		
War Diary	La Gorgue	07/04/1916	07/04/1916
War Diary	Riez Bailleul	11/04/1916	30/04/1916
War Diary	Mametz	01/05/1916	07/05/1916
War Diary	Vignacourt	30/05/1916	30/05/1916
War Diary	St Riquier	01/06/1915	01/06/1915
War Diary	Vignacourt	13/06/1916	13/06/1916
War Diary	Molliens-Aux-Bois	14/06/1916	17/06/1916
War Diary	Millencourt	23/06/1916	23/06/1916
War Diary	Carible?	28/06/1916	28/06/1916
Heading	8th Battn The North Staffordshire Regiment. July 1916		
War Diary	Millencourt	30/06/1916	05/07/1916
War Diary	Albert	06/07/1916	31/07/1916
Miscellaneous	Appendices		
Miscellaneous	19 Division	13/07/1916	13/07/1916
Miscellaneous	G.O.C. 57th Brigade	11/07/1916	11/07/1916
Miscellaneous			
Map			
Heading	1/8th Battalion North Stafford Regiment August 1916		
War Diary	Becourt Wood	31/07/1916	31/07/1916
War Diary	Bresle	03/08/1916	03/08/1916
War Diary	L'Etoile	06/08/1916	31/08/1916
War Diary	Trenches	03/09/1916	04/09/1916
War Diary	Dranoutre	06/09/1916	06/09/1916
War Diary	Le Romarin	12/09/1916	12/09/1916
War Diary	Trenches	16/09/1916	16/09/1916
War Diary	Red Lodge	20/09/1916	27/09/1916
War Diary	Pradelles	03/10/1916	06/10/1916
War Diary	Theivres	07/10/1916	07/10/1916
War Diary	Bois De Warimont	09/10/1916	17/10/1916
War Diary	Warloy	21/10/1916	22/10/1916
War Diary	Trenches	24/10/1916	01/11/1916
War Diary	Danobe Trench	02/11/1916	02/11/1916
War Diary	Crucifix Corner Near Avelov	03/11/1916	08/11/1916
War Diary	Trenches	09/11/1916	12/11/1916
War Diary	Marlborough Huts	13/11/1916	17/11/1916
War Diary	Regina Trench	18/11/1916	19/11/1916

War Diary	Marl Borough Huts	20/11/1916	22/11/1916
War Diary	Warloy	23/11/1916	24/11/1916
War Diary	Herrisart	25/11/1916	25/11/1916
War Diary	Fieffes	26/11/1916	26/11/1916
War Diary	St Ouen	27/11/1916	27/11/1916
War Diary	Longuevill	29/11/1916	30/11/1916
War Diary	Longuevillette	01/12/1916	31/12/1916
Heading	8th N Stafford Vol 8		
War Diary	Longuevillette	01/01/1917	09/01/1917
War Diary	Authieul	10/01/1917	10/01/1917
War Diary	Sailly Au-Bois And Hebuterne Keep	11/01/1917	14/01/1917
War Diary	In Trenches	15/01/1917	22/01/1917
War Diary	Courcelles	23/01/1917	31/01/1917
War Diary	Courcelles Au-Bois	01/02/1917	06/02/1917
War Diary	Trenches	07/02/1917	09/02/1917
War Diary	Trenches Sector L1	10/02/1917	11/02/1917
War Diary	Bus And Bertrancourt	12/02/1917	13/02/1917
War Diary	Bus Bertrancourt And Trenches	15/02/1917	17/02/1917
War Diary	Bertrancourt And Bus	18/02/1917	18/02/1917
War Diary	Bus and Bertrancourt	19/02/1917	24/02/1917
War Diary	Trenches	25/02/1917	27/02/1917
War Diary	Courcelles	28/02/1917	08/03/1917
War Diary	Courcelles & Louvencourt	09/03/1917	09/03/1917
War Diary	Louvencourt and Gezaincourt	10/03/1917	10/03/1917
War Diary	Gezaincourt and Bonniers	11/03/1917	11/03/1917
War Diary	Bonniers	12/03/1917	12/03/1917
War Diary	Bonniers and Croisette & Wignacourt	13/03/1917	13/03/1917
War Diary	Croisette Wignacourt & Hestrus	14/03/1917	14/03/1917
War Diary	Hestrus	15/03/1917	15/03/1917
War Diary	Equedecques & Lespresses	16/03/1917	16/03/1917
War Diary	Equedecques Lespresses & Thinnes	17/03/1917	17/03/1917
War Diary	Thinnes & Merris	18/03/1917	18/03/1917
War Diary	Merris	19/03/1917	20/03/1917
War Diary	Merris & Ridgewood	21/03/1917	21/03/1917
War Diary	Ridgewood & Trenches	22/03/1917	22/03/1917
War Diary	Trenches	23/03/1917	26/03/1917
War Diary	Ridgewood La Clyette	27/03/1917	27/03/1917
War Diary	Ridgewood & La Clyette	28/03/1917	29/03/1917
War Diary	Ridgewood & La Clyette and Phincboom	30/03/1917	30/03/1917
War Diary	Phincboom	31/03/1917	31/03/1917
Heading	57 Infy Bde Herewith War Diary for April 1917		
War Diary	Phincboom	01/04/1917	01/04/1917
War Diary	Phincboom & Hazebrouch	02/04/1917	03/04/1917
War Diary	Hazebrouch and St Martin-Au-Laert	03/04/1917	03/04/1917
War Diary	St Martin au Laert and Setques	04/04/1917	04/04/1917
War Diary	Setques & Moringhem Gd & Pt Difques	05/04/1917	05/04/1917
War Diary	Moringhem Gd & P.T Difques	06/04/1917	16/04/1917
War Diary	Moringhem Gd & P.T Difques and St Martin Au Laert	17/04/1917	17/04/1917
War Diary	Moringhem Gd & P.T Difques St Martin Au Laert and Hazebrouch	18/04/1917	18/04/1917
War Diary	Moringhem Gd & P.T Difques St Martin Au Laert and Hazebrouch and De Zon Camp	19/04/1917	23/04/1917
War Diary	Moringhem Gd & P.T Difques St Martin Au Laert and Hazebrouch De Zon Camp and Bethen	24/04/1917	25/04/1917
War Diary	De. Zon Camp	25/04/1917	29/04/1917
War Diary	De. Zon Camp and Scottish Camp G 23.A.8.6	30/04/1917	30/04/1917

War Diary	Scottish Lines G23 A 8.6	01/05/1917	01/05/1917
War Diary	Belgium & France 28 1/40,000 Scottish Lines & Trenches	02/05/1917	02/05/1917
War Diary	Trenches	03/05/1917	10/05/1917
War Diary	Scottish Lines & Weston Camp	11/05/1917	11/05/1917
War Diary	Weston Camp	12/05/1917	20/05/1917
War Diary	Morrumbridgee Camp	21/05/1917	24/05/1917
War Diary	Ridge Wood Morrum Bridgee Camp Trenches	25/05/1917	25/05/1917
War Diary	Trenches	26/05/1917	29/05/1917
War Diary	Trenches & Kempton Camp	30/05/1917	30/05/1917
War Diary	Kempton Camp	31/05/1917	31/05/1917
War Diary	Kempton Park Camp	01/06/1917	01/06/1917
War Diary	Map Reference Belgium France Sheet 28	02/06/1917	02/06/1917
War Diary	Edition 3 M 14 b 9.7 1/40,000	03/06/1917	05/06/1917
War Diary	Edition M 14 b 9.7 1/40,000 and Assembly area M12b1.9	06/06/1917	06/06/1917
War Diary	Reference Wyschaete 28 S.W. 1/10,000	07/06/1917	07/06/1917
War Diary	Reference Wyschaete	07/06/1917	08/06/1917
War Diary	Wytschaete	08/06/1917	10/06/1917
War Diary	France 28 SW 5a Edition	11/06/1917	12/06/1917
War Diary	Weston Camp M17d 77	13/06/1917	14/06/1917
War Diary	15/6/N	15/06/1917	17/06/1917
War Diary	Oosttaverne Sector 016 Ord O 22a06	18/06/1917	19/06/1917
War Diary	R24 a 0.5	20/06/1917	30/06/1917
War Diary	Stafford Camp R 24 W 0.5 N 17a 26	01/07/1917	02/07/1917
War Diary	Wytschaete 28 S W	03/07/1917	03/07/1917
War Diary	1/10000 Edition 5 A	04/07/1917	11/07/1917
War Diary	Wytschaete SW 1/10000	11/07/1917	11/07/1917
War Diary	Edition 5A Camp	12/07/1917	12/07/1917
War Diary	Siege Fm	13/07/1917	23/07/1917
War Diary	Wytschaete SW 1/10,000	24/07/1917	25/07/1917
War Diary	Edition 5 PE	26/07/1917	31/07/1917
War Diary	Ref. Map. France & Belg Sh. 28	01/08/1917	01/08/1917
War Diary	Beaver Corner 28.N.15.c.9.9	02/08/1917	02/08/1917
War Diary	Trenches 28.0.10 & 11	03/08/1917	05/08/1917
War Diary	Trenches	05/08/1917	06/08/1917
War Diary	Beaver Corner 28 N.15.c.9.9	07/08/1917	07/08/1917
War Diary	Ref. Map. Fr. Sheet 27 Stafford Camp 27 R 24.a.0.5	08/08/1917	10/08/1917
War Diary	Ref. Maps Haz.5.A. Calais. 13 Quesques	11/08/1917	21/08/1917
War Diary	Quesques Bellebrune	22/08/1917	22/08/1917
War Diary	Bellebrune	23/08/1917	27/08/1917
War Diary	Le Nieppe	28/08/1917	28/08/1917
War Diary	Moolenacker	29/08/1917	30/08/1917
Miscellaneous	Appendix A Roll Of Officers During Month		
Miscellaneous	Appendix B Monthly Roll Of Casualties		
War Diary	Appendix c	21/08/1917	21/08/1917
War Diary	Ref Sheet 27 Moolenacker	02/08/1917	05/08/1917
War Diary	Sheet 28 Epsom Camp Westoutre M146.11	06/08/1917	09/08/1917
War Diary	Bois Confluent Trenches I 35.6	10/08/1917	13/08/1917
War Diary	Boisconfluent	14/08/1917	14/08/1917
War Diary	Kemmel Shelters	15/08/1917	18/08/1917
War Diary	Trenches 1 Mile E Lys of Hill 60	19/08/1917	20/08/1917
War Diary	Trenches	20/08/1917	21/08/1917
War Diary	Kemmel Shelters	22/08/1917	30/08/1917
War Diary	Left Front Sector	01/10/1917	01/10/1917
War Diary	Trenches	02/10/1917	05/10/1917

War Diary	Clem Camp N 206.85.90	06/10/1917	10/10/1917
War Diary	Spoil Bank	11/10/1917	13/10/1917
War Diary	Left Front Sector	14/10/1917	14/10/1917
War Diary	Trenches	15/10/1917	17/10/1917
War Diary	Support	18/10/1917	19/10/1917
War Diary	Bois Confluent	20/10/1917	27/10/1917
War Diary	Clem Camp	28/10/1917	29/10/1917
War Diary	Tournai Camp	30/10/1917	01/11/1917
War Diary	Vierstraat	01/10/1917	04/11/1917
War Diary	Trenches	05/10/1917	07/11/1917
War Diary	In Suffort	08/11/1917	09/11/1917
War Diary	Moolenacker	10/11/1917	11/11/1917
War Diary	Le Croquet	12/11/1917	27/11/1917
War Diary	Cormette	28/10/1917	30/10/1917
War Diary	Campagne SE of Stomer	01/12/1917	06/12/1917
War Diary	Pommier	07/12/1917	08/12/1917
War Diary	Etricourt Trenches Map Ref Nine Wood 1/10,000	08/12/1917	09/12/1917
War Diary	Hindenburg Line	10/12/1917	10/12/1917
War Diary	Trenches	11/12/1917	14/12/1917
War Diary	Hindenburg Line	15/12/1917	15/12/1917
War Diary	Hindenburg Line Map Ref Nine Wood 1/10,000	16/12/1917	20/12/1917
War Diary	Havrincourt Wood	21/12/1917	22/12/1917
War Diary	Map Ref Nine Wood 1/10,000	22/12/1917	22/12/1917
War Diary	Trenches	23/12/1917	29/12/1917
War Diary	Map Ref Nine Wood 1/10,000	30/12/1917	31/12/1917
War Diary	Map Ref Nine Wood 1/10,000 Trenches	31/12/1917	06/01/1918
War Diary	Ninewood 1/10,000	06/01/1918	07/01/1918
War Diary	Vallulart Camp	08/01/1918	12/01/1918
War Diary	1/10,000 Nine Wood	13/01/1918	21/01/1918
War Diary	Eastwood Camp	22/01/1918	22/01/1918
War Diary	Trenches	23/01/1918	23/01/1918
War Diary	Nine Wood 1/10,000	23/01/1918	31/01/1918

WO95/20852

19TH DIVISION
57TH INFY BDE

8TH BN NTH STAFFS.
JLY 1915 - JAN 1918

To 56 BDE. 19 DIV

57th Inf.Bde.
19th Div.

Battn. disembarked
Havre from England
18.7.15.

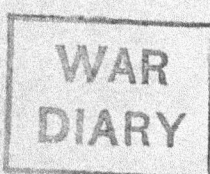

8th BATTN. THE NORTH STAFFORDSHIRE REGIMENT.

J U L Y
(17.7.15 - 31.7.15)
1 9 1 5
to
Jan '18

Army Form C. 2118

8th N. Stafford Sheet I

WAR DIARY
INTELLIGENCE SUMMARY
(Erase heading not required.)

Instructions regarding War Diaries and Intelligence Summaries are contained in F.S. Regs., Part II. and the Staff Manual respectively. Title Pages will be prepared in manuscript.

Place	Date	Hour	Summary of Events and Information	Remarks and references to Appendices
Southampton	17/7/15	7.30PM	Embarked	ad
HAVRE	18/7/15	7AM	Disembarked. Left for front 4.30 PM 20/7/15 by train	ad
Audriey	21/7/15	3.30PM	Disembarked from train, marched 8 miles to Mentque + Nortbecourt, billets.	ad
NORTBECOURT	23/7/15	7AM	Marched in Brigade to RENESCURE, arrived 4.30PM, via MOULLE + St OMER. Smoke helmets were issued, + later it was found that the tube windows broke easily, if care was not taken in folding them correctly. Good village for billeting.	ad
RENESCURE	24/7/15	7AM	Marched in Brigade to MOLINGHEM, arrived 2PM, via AIRE, billets.	ad
MOLINGHEM	25/7/15	5PM	Inspected in billets by Sir DOUGLAS HAIGH	ad
"	30/7/15	9.30AM	Marched in Brigade to HAVERSKERQUE arrived 12.30 PM, billets.	ad
MERVILLE	31/7/15	12.30PM	Marched from HAVERSKERQUE arrived 3.30PM in INDIAN CORPS RESERVE billets in vicinity of MERVILLE. During march from detraining station to join corps a large number of men suffered from sore feet, due almost entirely to the fact that new boots were issued just before leaving England.	ad

57th Inf.Bde.
19th Div.

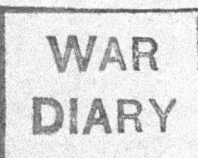

8th BATTN. THE NORTH STAFFORDSHIRE REGIMENT.

A U G U S T

(2.8.15 - 29.8.15)

1 9 1 5

INTELLIGENCE SUMMARY

(Erase heading not required.)

Sheet II

Place	Date	Hour	Summary of Events and Information	Remarks and references to Appendices
near MERVILLE	2/8/15	12 noon	The Bn was inspected by Sir JAMES WILLCOCKS. About this time it was found that the two water-carts issued to the Bn were found to be temporarily unserviceable, owing to jolting on the line of march. The defect was in the pumping apparatus & connections to tank. The carts were of the 1915 pattern mark V. The pumps had only been used once under personal supervision of M.O.	AdS
ESTAIRES	11/8/15	5 pm	Arrived from last billet, marching as a Bn. Billets. The 5 water tanks issued were found to be fitted with a mica window, which broke rather easily. To prevent this, thin pieces of wood were bought, & the window fitted round this.	AdS
TRENCHES	12/8/15	5-10pm	marched by Coys from billets from LA BASSÉ road & billets. Highlanders to be increased. Water supply very bad.	AdS
			D Coy; in trenches had large minenwerfer shell on parapet. Blew down 30 yds. has 14 rifles & several packs buried in debris. Shewed need for trench pails.	AdS
	13th – 14th		D Coy came out & C Coy went into trenches with 1st Seaforths	
	night of		B Coy also went into trenches with 4th Seaforths	AdS
	night of 16th-17th		B & C Coys came out of trenches, & A Coy went into them with 4th Seaforths.	AdS
	17th		From experience it was found that rations sent to trenches should be put in small bags not weighing more than 40 lbs, so that one man can carry them up communicating trenches. Empty tins of small size are also useful for storing water	AdS

SHEET III

INTELLIGENCE SUMMARY
(Erase heading not required.)

Instructions regarding War Diaries and Intelligence Summaries are contained in F.S. Regs, Part II. and the Staff Manual respectively. Title Pages will be prepared in manuscript.

Place	Date	Hour	Summary of Events and Information	Remarks and references to Appendices
TRENCHES	17.8.15	2 pm	"D" Coy marched to the old billets in vicinity of MERVILLE, occupied by us from 31/7/15 to 14/8/15	as
"	18.8.15	3 pm	"C" Coy also marched to the old billets near MERVILLE.	as
"	19.8.15	2.30pm	The remainder of the Bn followed. The 9th WELCH REGT reoccupied our billets as we passed them.	as
"			During the tour in the trenches, there were men were hit by the enemy, & two accidental casualties occurred.	as
MERVILLE	21/8/15	4 pm	D Coy furnished a party of 200 men, having 32 from C Coy to make up numbers, for a working party at the trenches. A similar number from the 8th & 9th R Regt went with them, the whole under a Major of the Gloster Regt. They did not take Greatcoats, Gas Sign etc.	as
"	25/8/15	2.30pm	The working party mentioned above returned. Casualties, one officer, 2 Lt F. G. Gadsby wounded, he was evidently sniped from behind our lines, from the nature of the wound.	as
"	24/8/15	11.30 am	While practising with live bombs, an accident occurred, killing one man & mortally wounding another. This was the first accident with bombs in the Bn.	as
"	27/8/15	3.45pm	marched as Bn from Billets & went into billets at PARADIS.	as
PARADIS	28/8/15	5.45pm	marched as Bn from billets to position in Brigade Reserve for our section of trenches. "A" Coy going into local reserve to 10th WORCESTER REGT. "B" Coy garrisoning Keppes & posts, "C" & "D" Coys & HQ in billets on KINGS ROAD.	as

Sheet IV

INTELLIGENCE SUMMARY

(Erase heading not required.)

Place	Date	Hour	Summary of Events and Information	Remarks and references to Appendices
TRENCHES	29/8/15		"A" Coy came out about 10 P.M., owing to re-arrangement of Bns, & reoccupied billets in KINGS ROAD.	All

57th Inf.Bde.
19th Div.

WAR DIARY

8th BATTN. THE NORTH STAFFORDSHIRE REGIMENT.

S E P T E M B E R
(2.9.15 - 29.9.15)
1 9 1 5

Attached:

Appendices I & II.

SHEET V

INTELLIGENCE SUMMARY

(Erase heading not required.)

Place	Date	Hour	Summary of Events and Information	Remarks and references to Appendices
TRENCHES	17/9/15	7.30pm	Went into firing line of trenches in INDIA II A section, occupying a salient called The CANADIAN ORCHARD. Were subjected to continual & persistent bombardment from the enemy, with High Explosives, minenwerfers, & bombs.	I Account of any gallantry brought to notice of G.O.C. 57th Bde.
"	19/9/15	11.15pm	We were relieved by 7th KING'S OWN REGT, & left the trenches marching to the relieving regt billets at LOCON. The Bn: was congratulated by G.O.C. 57th BDE on its cheerfulness & fortitude under trying circumstances. Casualties in the trenches were 10 Killed 35 wounded.	II Plan of trenches in Salient CANADIAN SALIENT. AS
LOCON	21/9/15		Up to this date were in rest billets, where we received orders to hold ourselves in readiness to move in Corps reserve when ordered.	AS
"	20/9/15		Received a draft of 25 N.C.O's & men.	AS
"	{25/9/15 2.40pm / 27/9/15}		Marched to LE HAMEL and also to one mile W of GORRE, being in Army Reserve during the offensive movement commencing on 25/9/15	AS
LE HAMEL	29/9/15	5.30pm	Having returned to LE HAMEL, received orders to relieve 58th BDE. This nyt: relieved 6th WILTSHIRE REGT in trenches IND IB opposite FESTUBERT & LE PLANTIN	AS

Aug 8th N. Shaffer Pt/L

APPENDICES

I & II

Confidential.   57th Brigade   I

I wish to bring the following officer & men to
the notice of the G.O.C for conspicuous bravery
        Captain R F WYNNE
  No 14174   Pte JOHNSON F
  No 16878   "   BREEZE J.W.
  No 17240   "   HEMMINGS E

On the morning of 11th Sept about 8.30 am during
a bombardment of our front trenches by the enemy
L. Cpl Berrisford was lifted clean out of the trench
by the explosion of an HE Shell & thrown across
our wire about 25 yards in front on the German
side — where he hung.

Capt Wynne & the three above mentioned men
without hesitation went over the parapet & although
they had to send back for wire cutters to disentangle
L. Cpl Berrisford — succeeded in bringing him
back into our own trench still alive. The wire
at this point is not more than 85 yards from
the German front line & our whole line of trenches
were at the time under a heavy artillery &
trench mortar fire.

L. Cpl Berrisford unfortunately died soon after
he was brought back into our trench.

                W.T. Lockur Lt Col.
                Comd 8th N Stafford Regt.

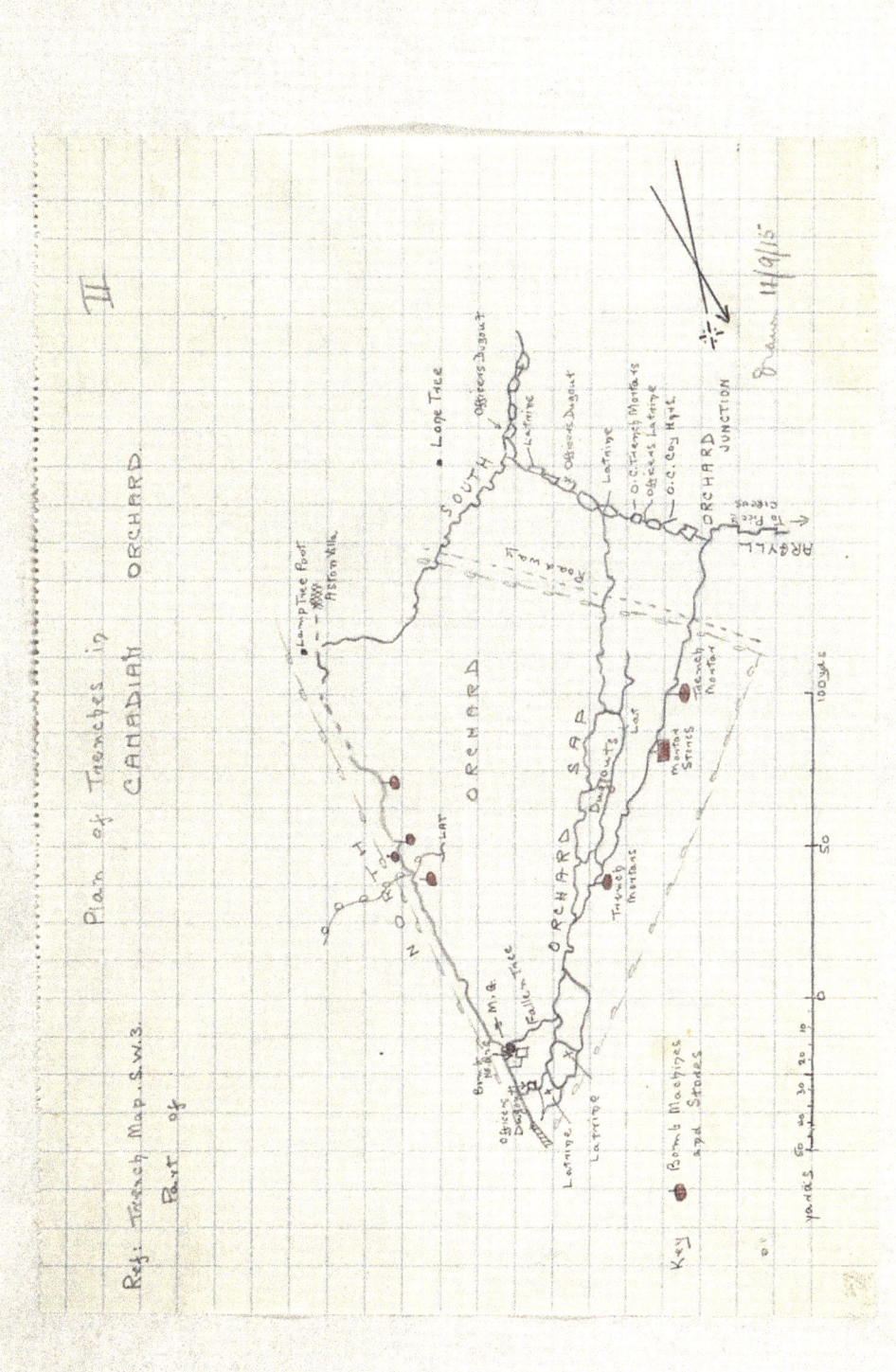

57th Inf.Bde.
19th Div.

8th BATTN. THE NORTH STAFFORDSHIRE REGIMENT.

O C T O B E R

(29.9.15 - 1.11.15)

1 9 1 5

WAR DIARY
INTELLIGENCE SUMMARY
(Erase heading not required.)

Sheet VI

Instructions regarding War Diaries and Intelligence Summaries are contained in F.S. Regs., Part II. and the Staff Manual respectively. Title Pages will be prepared in manuscript.

Place	Date	Hour	Summary of Events and Information	Remarks and references to Appendices
Trenches	29/9/15		Went into Ins VI B section trenches opposite FESTUBERT. Relieved 6th Wilts. Trenches very bad owing to 3 days rain.	
	30/9/15		Extended front about 200x to left, taking in part of ROTHESAY BAY. During past night ½ 30th – 1st brought in and buried bodies of 5 Wilts men & one R. Welsh Fusiliers, buried bodies behind Sap 15.	
	2/10/15		Relieved by 1st SEAFORTHS, & went back to LE HAMEL.	
	3/10/15		Went into Ins VI B section, relieving 89th PUNJABIS, FEROZEPORE BDE.	
	5/10/15		About 3 A.M., heavy bombardment with H.E. & shrapnel by enemy. Lasted about ¾ hour. No damage done. Spent most of these days cleaning trenches	
	7/10/15		10th Worcester Regt. took over 8 traverses from us, on our right. Killed a German sniper today, & a few days later hope a large enemy periscope.	
	11/10/15		Were relieved by 8th Gloucester Regt, went into billets about 2 miles back. A Coy holding posts & Keeps round Dead Cow & Chocolate Posts, & C Coy holding those about Richebourg Post. Moved H.Q. & remainder of C Coy to the village of RICHEBOURG St VAAST, remainder of Bn being in Reserve Trenches.	
	13/10/15		During this evening, enemy fired some shells into the village, which on exploding caused our eyes to smart & smart.	
	15/10/15		Moved into Reserve about LACOUTURE, 10th R. Warr. Regt. taking our place, & we took billets over from 10th Worcester Regt.	

Sheet VII

INTELLIGENCE SUMMARY
(Erase heading not required.)

Instructions regarding War Diaries and Intelligence Summaries are contained in F.S. Regs., Part II. and the Staff Manual respectively. Title Pages will be prepared in manuscript.

Place	Date	Hour	Summary of Events and Information	Remarks and references to Appendices
Lacouture	16/10/15 to 20/10/15		At rest in billets. Had about 10 H.E. shells near us. Took over trenches from native infantry troops, & relieved them in 53 minutes, a record relief so far.	
Trenches In 2 / B Sub-section	20/10/15 to 1/11/15		Enemy very quiet in our front, hardly replying to our sniping & gun fire. Got plenty of rain this tour, the trenches getting in very bad state; dug-outs, parapets & traverses falling in; the liquid mud being up to ones knees.	

× measured 1/11/15
in weasel [?]

W. J. Lockie, Lieut.
Ad. Offr. n. Staffs Regt.

57th Inf.Bde.
19th Div.

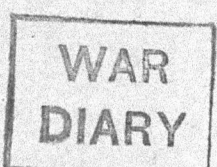

8th BATTN. THE NORTH STAFFORDSHIRE REGIMENT.

N O V E M B E R

(5.11.15 - 25.11.15)

1 9 1 5

Sheet VIII

WAR DIARY
INTELLIGENCE SUMMARY
(Erase heading not required.)

Place	Date	Hour	Summary of Events and Information	Remarks and references to Appendices
LE HAMEL	5/11/15		Went into the trenches IND 1b, opposite Festubert cross Roads on Quinque Rue, relieving 10th Worcesters. Trenches in very bad condition, owing to rain. Many traverses down, & the communication trenches absolutely impassable. In the foggy morning's caught several enemy working parties, both with artillery fire, & m.g., rifle fire. Casualties two killed & two wounded. 5 & 6th B.R. were on our left & 10th R.R. on our right, out in the open. Enemy busy digging & improving their own men.	
LOCON	10/11/15		Relieved last night by 7th R.Q.R. Lancaster Regt, 57th B.R., forwards back to Locon, in pelting rain.	
	13/11/15	10 am	Battn. Inspected by Major Gen Jackson C.B. commanding 19th Division	
RUE DU BOIS	17/11/15	5 pm	Took over post & trenches from 9th Q.W.F. in Rue de L'Epinette in Bn in IV Reserve	
TRENCHES	21/11/15		Took over IND 2 & 6 from 6th Gloucester Regt. 5b & 13th on our right & 139 Bde ... Div on our left. The worst bit of line we have yet had. No parapet left in many parts. Support parapet only about 2'6" high - wire absolutely insufficient everywhere. Communication at parts on the open & and at night. Casualties during 3 days in trenches. 2 killed & 5 wounded.	
"	24/11/15		Handed over sub-sector to 5th London Regt. Relief finished about 9.30 pm - marched back old billets at LOCON.	
LOCON	25/11/15	10 am	Marched to XI Corps Rest billets near ROGER.	

W Mather Lt Col
Commanding 2nd Staffords

57th Inf.Bde.
19th Div.

8th BATTN. THE NORTH STAFFORDSHIRE REGIMENT.

D E C E M B E R

(29.11.15 - 31.12.15)

1 9 1 5

Sheet IX

WAR DIARY
INTELLIGENCE SUMMARY
(Erase heading not required.)

Place	Date	Hour	Summary of Events and Information	Remarks and references to Appendices
ROBECQ	29/11/15		"D" Coy was inspected by Major General HAKIN comdg XI Corps.	
"	4/12/15		Bn. marched to billets at C'tx MARMUSE, found that 56th Dn. had not recced our proposed billets, so took what we could in neighbourhood. Roads frequently well over boot tops in water.	
C'tx MARMUSE	5/12/15		Got into own billets today.	
"	10/12/15		Brig: Gen: TWYFORD inspects the Bn.	
"	11/12/15		Marched to billets in King's Road from R. Welsh Fusiliers. Bde. in trenches, 10th Worcester Regt & 8th Gloucesters up in front line.	
KING'S ROAD	13/12/15		Went into trenches in relief of 8th Gloucesters, trenches mostly under water, line held by small posts or islands. Bn firing active, enemy retaliating over near CORNER inclusive. Line held by us extended from QUINQUE RUE to FARM CORNER inclusive. 10th R. Warwick Regt on our left. Frequent patrols on our front reporting enemy working parties, & enemy snipers fairly alert.	
	19/12/15		Relieved by 8th Gloster Regt. went back to old billets in King's Road. During tour, had one coy of Bn HQ of 13th Welsh Regt attached for instruction. They left on 20/12/15, were replaced by one coy of 14th Welsh Regt.	

INTELLIGENCE SUMMARY

Sheet X

(Erase heading not required.)

Instructions regarding War Diaries and Intelligence Summaries are contained in F.S. Regs., Part II. and the Staff Manual respectively. Title Pages will be prepared in manuscript.

Place	Date	Hour	Summary of Events and Information	Remarks and references to Appendices
KINGS ROAD	23/12/15		Relieved 8th Gloucesters Regt in trenches, same dispositions as last time. Frequent patrols had same reports to make as last time. Heavy shelling on Trenches + near Bn HQ. on occasions.	
	27/12/15		Relieved by 58th BDE, 7th N. LANC REGT. & marched to billets on LE TOURET – LACOUTURE ROAD.	
LE TORET	31/12/15		Inspected by Gen: Bridges Cmdg 19th DIVN. who expressed himself as very pleased with the way the men turned out	

W.L. Walker
Lt Col
Cmdg 8th N Stafford Regt.

Sir H. Stafford
vol: 7

Temple

19

Army Form C. 2118

Sheet XI

5th N. Staffs Regt

WAR DIARY
or
INTELLIGENCE SUMMARY
(Erase heading not required.)

Instructions regarding War Diaries and Intelligence Summaries are contained in F.S. Regs., Part II. and the Staff Manual respectively. Title Pages will be prepared in manuscript.

Place	Date	Hour	Summary of Events and Information	Remarks and references to Appendices
Le Touret	4/1/16		Marched to CROIX-BARBÉE, going into billets, the 8th R. War. R. being in billets also. 10th Worc. Regt & 8th Gloster Regt in front line.	
CROIX-BARBÉE	8/1/16		Relieved 8th Gloster Regt in trenches, 10th R. War. R. on our left, & 15th R. Welsh Fusiliers on our right. 9th & 113th Bde. During this tour of the trenches, 9th Welsh Regt came up, 50 Nee's gun came up with H officers & carried out two simultaneous bombing attacks on points where guns had sent enemy wire. No prisoners were brought back, but casualties to enemy uncertain. At dawn next morning, we made a feint attack with smoke bombs at 7 A.M. from our right coy. guns put up a barrage on enemy support lines at same time. The Hooken approached him to bring fire on our parapet, particularly through bursting on pas kilomets, & at no time was his rifle & M.G. fire heavy, shewing that his line is thinly held. Our patrols brought in useful information about enemy Popes horn & some of his new works S.E. of Bois du Rue du Bois, Richebourg & Laventure. Enemy reply by gun fire was moderate, but he retaliated later on our MG.	
"	12/1/16		Relieved by 8th Glosters, returned to billets in Croix Barbée.	
"	17/1/16		Relieved 8th Glosters in trenches, 5 8th Batt on our right, 10th R. War. Regt on our left. No XI Trench Mortar Battery was in line with us, & in 3 days, fired about 100 rounds at enemy	

1875 Wt. W593/826 1,000,000 4/15 J.B.C. & A. A.D.S.S./Forms/C. 2118.

8 N. Stafford

Army Form C. 2118.
Sheet XII

WAR DIARY
or
INTELLIGENCE SUMMARY
(Erase heading not required.)

Instructions regarding War Diaries and Intelligence Summaries are contained in F.S. Regs., Part II. and the Staff Manual respectively. Title Pages will be prepared in manuscript.

Place	Date	Hour	Summary of Events and Information	Remarks and references to Appendices
CROIX-BARBÉE	29/1/16		parapet, breaking it in 2 cases well, + not to well in a third case. Enemy brought up small trench mortars in reply on 3rd day, but did no very great harm. He also sent over rifle grenades & small bombs apparently shot from trench guns. We replied with rifle grenades. Enemy almost invariably retaliated for our guns fire & trench mortar fire on Bn HQ, + Port Arthur Redpt; Bn HQ being on Rue du Bois, with an artillery O.P. about 20 yds to left front. On one occasion it was shelled heavily for 1½ hours. Total casualties during this tour, including two days return & day were up in trenches with 8th Glosters Regt 1 Officer (2Lt W.H. Lucas) 7 killed, 14 wounded.	
"	29/1/16		Relieved by 10th Welsh Regt 11th Bde. Went into billets at Croix-Barbée. Marched to old billets in RODEEQ, being relieved by 13th Welsh Regt at Croix-Barbée.	
RODEEQ	29/1/16		Attaching original letter from 19th Div: received, & communicated to all ranks.	
	31/1/16		Started training on Monday 31st —, with short marches drill order, Physical Training, musketry, + lectures on various subjects.	

Wilochen
[signature]
Cmdg 8th N. Stafford Regt.

C O P Y.

19th. Division. No. 1G.4.905.

Headquarters,
 57th. Brigade.

The Divisional Commander wishes to convey to you and to all ranks serving under you his appreciation of the work which has been done during the last tour of your Brigade in the trenches. The improvement in the trenches and defences generally which has taken place during this period is most marked and reflects great credit on all ranks.

H.Q. 19th. Division. (Sd) P.M. Johnson Lt.Col. G.S.
23rd. January 1916.   19th. Division.

(2)

To:-
 The Officer Commanding,
  8th. North Staffordshire Regt.

It gives the G.O.C. Brigade much pleasure to forward the above letter to Officers Commanding Battalions for communication to all ranks.

D A Bower Cpl
for Brigade Major,
57th. Infantry Brigade.

24/1/16.

19.

8. N Staffs
Vol 9

Army Form C. 2118

Sheet XIII

WAR DIARY
or
8th N. Stafford Regt
INTELLIGENCE SUMMARY

(Erase heading not required.)

Instructions regarding War Diaries and Intelligence Summaries are contained in F. S. Regs., Part II. and the Staff Manual respectively. Title Pages will be prepared in manuscript.

Place	Date	Hour	Summary of Events and Information	Remarks and references to Appendices
ROBECQ	1/2/16		Bn Training was continued, progressing from marches by platoons, to Coys, & finally Bn Route marches. A system of wiring in front of own trenches was demonstrated by 5th S.W.B. (Pioneers), & this was taught to the Bn, to be put into execution when we went into the trenches.	
"	19/2/16		Bde marched to billets in La Gorgue & Merville. 8th Gloster Regt being at La Gorgue, 10th R. War. Regt & ourselves being close to Merville. Bde HR are in La Gorgue. We took over billets formerly occupied by part of Guards Div.	
MERVILLE	24/2/16		Bn marched from Merville to billets in RIEZ BAILLEUL, these billets being vacated by 9th R.W.F. (58th BDE). Bn is in reserve to 8th Glosters who are in the line, 10th R. War. Regt billeted on Le Barat Rd at Pont du Hem, being in reserve to 10th Worc: Regt in the line.	
RIEZ BAILLEUL	24/2/16		Relieved 8th Gloucesters in the trenches, 10th R. War. R. on our left. As these relief were only in two days & 2 days out, very little can be done, either in work or strapping the Hun.	
"	25/2/16		Came out of trenches, relieved by 8th Gloucesters. Went back into old billets at Riez Bailleul	

Signed L.Col
Cmdg 8th N Stafford Regt

Army Form C. 2118

Sheet XIV

WAR DIARY
INTELLIGENCE SUMMARY

8th (S) Bn North or South Staffs Regt

(Erase heading not required.)

Place	Date	Hour	Summary of Events and Information	Remarks and references to Appendices
RIEZ BAILLEUL	3/3/16		Relieved 8th Gloucesters in the trenches, leaving from Gonnehem, having travelled to the old system of 4 days in & 4 days out. This turn of the trenches was nearly dry, very cold weather, snow, sleet & freezing at night. A thaw in the day caused flooding in the trenches. In the "Duck's Bill", we bombarded the enemy with 90 Rifle Grenades; he did not retaliate till the last 50. The Artillery fired on a pump in his lines, & the enemy promptly retaliated. Patrol work was rather difficult sometimes owing to the snow, so we were wiring; but a fair amount was done. We bombed out our own dummy listening post.	
" "	7/3/16		Relieved by 17th Royal Scots (Bantam Bn) and 19th D.L.I. (Bantams) were attached to us. Five frog containers were tried, for conveying hot soup, cocoa etc to the front line. They were little large thermos flasks. (four men carried them up from Holly Hed, when they arrived full with the rations nightly. If they were kept filled with hot water during the day), & the soup or cocoa served in really hot up to the last moment, they proved a great blessing to the men in the trenches. Proceeded that night to billets in La Gorgue. It snowed the whole night; a fine wet snow that did not lay. Casualties this period in the trenches, Lt Langley & wounded, other ranks 2 killed, ten wounded. During the last period 9th the trenches,	

1875 Wt. W593/826 1,000,000 4/15 J.B.C. & A. A.D.S.S./Forms/C. 2118.

Army Form C. 2118

Sheet XV

WAR DIARY
8t(S) Bn North. Staffordshire Regt.
INTELLIGENCE SUMMARY
(Erase heading not required.)

Place	Date	Hour	Summary of Events and Information	Remarks and references to Appendices
La Gorgue	15/3/16		Marched from La Gorgue to old billets in Rue Bailleul, taking them over from 8th Gloucesters, who went up into the line with 10th R.W.F. R on their left. Wire in La Gorgue; found large working & wiring parties, for a proposed scheme against the enemy. 2/Lt D.Y.A Line was wounded on 12th while on working party, and drowned on 13/3/16 while Bn was out of fatigue party; lost one N.C.O. killed, and P.K. wounded.	
Rue Bailleul	16/3/16		Practised A&D Coys. in g. Bombers in formations for the proposed raiding scheme. D Coy relieved one coy of 10th Worcester Regt in the trenches, getting it put to practise for the raid. Our working parties were specially commended by OC 2nd Field Coy R.E. for work done on night 16/17.	
"	17/3/16			
Rue Bailleul	20/3/16	10 pm	The large raid having abandoned the Bat. Bombers + 90 men of D Coy - the whole under the command of Capt. P.B. PURVES made a raid on the German front line opposite the BIRDCAGE near WINCHESTER Rd following the explosion of 5 9" mine. The raid was successful & some twenty fifths enemy were accounted for. The Bat. was congratulated by Bde Genl. Twyford cmdg 57th Inf Bde + got a special order + Copy of the above from platoon an attack+ G.O.R wounded. All our wounded were safely brought in	Appx A

Army Form C. 2118

WAR DIARY / INTELLIGENCE SUMMARY

8th (S) Batn. ~~of~~ North Stafford Regt.

Sheet XVI

(Erase heading not required.)

Place	Date	Hour	Summary of Events and Information	Remarks and references to Appendices
CHAPIGNY Section	21/3/16		Relieved 9th Gloucester Regt in front line – 59th Bde on our right – 10th R. War. R. on our left. The Ducks Bill had been blown up by a German mine + the enemy's lip of the crater was held by him.	
"	22/3/16	11.45pm	A German patrol attempted to approach the crater – it was trailed by one of our posts – I man being killed & 1 wounded. The dead German was brought in & subsequently buried in our cemetery.	
"	"		Our 8" guns endeavoured to wreck an enemy mine shaft near COLVIN. Result beyond of our parapet wrecked + a front stone exploded.	
"	23/3/16	6.30am	Enemy sprang a mine near COLVIN St – little damage to our parapet but he had 6 men killed + 1 officer (2nd Lieut WEST) & 31 OR wounded by falling debris. We occupy the nearer lip of the crater.	
"	24/3/16	10.30am to 5pm	Enemy bombarded our front line near SIGNPOST LANE & DUCKS BILL with heavy shells – our parapet was knocked in several places but we had no casualties.	
"	26/3/16		Relieved by 8th Gloucester R. & went into billets at RUE 3 BAILLEUL.	
"	29/3/16		Relieves 8th Gloucester in front line. 56th Bde on our right – 10th R. War R on our left.	
"	1/4/16		Relieved by 6th Cheshire Regt & returned to billets in Divisional Reserve at La Gorgue, taking over billets there from 12th Royal Sussex Regt.	

J Cannop Major
O.C. 8th North Stafford Regt.

S E C R E T   Operation Order No. 24.

LEFT GROUP 19th DIVISIONAL ARTILLERY.

OPERATION for NIGHT 20/21st MARCH 1916

OBJECT. 1. No.255 Mining Co. R.E. are exploding a series of mines about the line M.30.A.3.4. to M.30.A.5.5. This is timed for 10 p.m. and will be followed immediately by a bombing attack by 8th North Staffordshire Regt. up to and including the enemy trench M.30.A.4.3. to 6.5.
The Infantry action will be supported by the Left Group Artillery as follows:-

ACTION OF LEFT GROUP ARTILLERY. 2.

UNIT.	OBJECTIVE.	AMMUNITION.	TIMING.
B/159 18 pdr	Strong points at M.30.C.8.8.	60 Shrapnel	Slow fire from Mine going up to 10.45 p.m.
A/88 4.5" How.	Strong points at M.30.C.8.8.	30 H.E.	Slow fire from mine going up to 10.45 p.m.
A/159 18pdr Ho	Enfilade fire on Trench M.30.A.5.3. to 7.3.	90 H.E.	About 6 rounds per minute from 10.30 p.m. to 10.45 p.m.
D/159 18pdr	Enfilade fire on Trench M.30.A.7½.5. to 5½.5.	90 H.E.	About 6 rounds per minute from 10.30 p.m. to 10.45 p.m.

Should the Infantry Officer conducting the operation wish for the fire of A/159 & D/159 before 10.30 p.m. the demand for it will be sent back through Captain Heron. R.F.A. through Group Hqs.

T.M.Batteries & Mgs. 3. The action of T.M.Batteries and Mgs is shown in attached table A.

Communication 4. Capt. Heron attached to A/88th R.F.A. will establish communication from our front line trenches to Group Hq. and to Sec/Lt. Dickson B/88th R.F.A. who will move forward with the bombing party and establish telephone and if necessary lamp communication from the craters. Captain Heron and 2/Lieut Dickson will act as liason officers with the Infantry officer conducting the operations.

Official Time 5. Official time having been received from the 57th Inf. Brigade will be sent out at 7 p.m.
In accordance with instructions of G.O.C. 57th Inf. Brigade Captain Heron will communicate official time to the Infantry Officer conducting the operations, the officer 255th Mining Coy R.E. and T.M. Officers.

Telephone System 6. The telephone System in front of Group Hq. will be used tactical messages only from 9 p.m. until the conclusion of the operation.

Issued at ..... a.m.   Lt-Col. R.
20/3/16.   Commanding Left Group
                                                               19 ?

Copies to:-

War Diary

SPECIAL ORDER OF THE DAY
by
Major-General T. Bridges, C.M.G., D.S.O,
Commanding 19th Division.

23/3/16.

The General Officer Commanding desires to congratulate the Officers and men of the 8th (S) Battalion North Staffordshire Regiment for the daring enterprise which was carried out by them at short notice and under difficult circumstances on the night of the 20/21 March.

This offensive action had the desired effect of upsetting the enemy's nerves and caused him to prematurely spring a mine and to waste countless rounds of ammunition.

It must always be borne in mind that every offensive action, however, small, that is carried out with determination has an effect on the enemy's morale quite out of proportion to any casualties that we may inflict or suffer and has a direct influence on the comparative values of the opposing forces by raising our own morale and correspondingly lowering that of the enemy.

P.M.Davies, Lieut-Colonel,
A.A. & Q.M.G., 19th Division.

In War Diary

Copy of 11th Corps Wire No. G.842. dated 21/3/16.

19th Division.

Following from Army Commander begins :-
To :- Commander XIth Corps.
Am delighted to hear of your successful raid last night.
Please congratulate all concerned from me. This is just what we want.
From MONRO.

    11th Corps.

---

(2)

To :- The Officer Commanding

    10th R.WAR.R.   87th M.G.Coy.
    8th GLOUC.R.   X-19, Z.19 and No.71 T.M.Bs.
    10th WORC.R.   Nos.87/1 and 87/2 T.M.Bs.
    8th N.STAFF.R.

Forwarded for information of all concerned.

A.Raymond Captain,
for
Acting Brigade Major,
87th Infantry Brigade.

22/3/16.

O.C. 8 N. Staff. R.

INSTRUCTION AND INFORMATION RE MINOR OPERATIONS TO BE CARRIED OUT NIGHT of 20th/21st MARCH.

1. The operation formerly discussed and for which preliminary orders were issued are cancelled, and the following is substituted :-

2. Our mines under the German Salient M 30.a. Central will be exploded at 10 p.m. 20th March.

3. In conjunction with the explosion the 8th North Staffordshire Regt. will carry out a bombing raid on the German Salient.

4. The following arrangements will be made in the trenches, left Subsector by the O.C. Left Subsector.
   Bays occupied by 8th North Staffordshire Regt will be cleared as O.C., 8th North Staffordshire Regt. directs.
   Bays 32 to 50 inclusive will be cleared of 10th Royal Warwickshire Regt. to make room for the N. STAFF.R. bombing party.
   The Company H.Q. of 10th Royal Warwickshire Regt. near the junction of WINCHESTER C.T. and front line will be vacated and used for 8th North Staffordshire Regt. Headquarters and Communications.
   A party of 5 N.C.O's and 20 men from front Company, 10th Royal Warwickshire Regt. will report to the Adjutant, 8th North Staffordshire Regt. at junction of WINCHESTER C.T. and front line at 9 p.m. and will be detailed by him to escort any prisoners to Brigade H.Q.

5. Rapid fire from rifles and M.Gs. will be opened at 10 p.m. from our parapet M 24 c 9.1. Northwards and M 30 c 2.3. Southwards - this fire to be kept up for three minutes and afterwards for about one minute with five minutes intervals. Great care must be taken that all men in this line are instructed not to fire towards the German Salient during the operation.

6. Two parties of 82nd Company R.E. will accompany the Raiding Party of 8th North Staffordshire Regt to blow up enemy's mine shafts and emplacements etc. These to report to the Adjutant, 8th North Staffordshire Regt. at junction WINCHESTER C.T. and firing line at 9 p.m.

Official time to be checked by all parties at 8 p.m.

SCHEME FOR AN OFFENSIVE OPERATION TO BE CARRIED OUT ON 20/3/16.

Ref. GERMAN MAP 1/1000

1. Objects.
   (a). To raid the German trenches on N. side of his Salient and kill or capture Germans.

   (b). To sweep that portion of the German Salient which lies between the craters and the front line trench running from crater F to Pt 41.a. and kill or capture any Germans found there and generally take advantage of the effects of the explosion of our mines.

2. Troops employed.
   (a) A bombing party of 1 Officer and 27 other ranks.
   (b) A sweeping party of 1 Officer and 40 men.
   (c) A covering party of 1 Officer and 30 men.

   The whole under the Command of Captain P.B.Purves.

3. Scheme of attack.
   (a) The troops to be employed will be assembled in the fire trench in the left subsector - left Brigade from Bays 32 to 50 inclusive - after dark.
   (b) The signal for the advance will be the explosion of 5 mines at 10 P.M.
   (c) The bombing party will advance first, followed by the sweeping party at a distance of 30 yards. The covering party will advance as soon as the sweeping party has reached the near edge of the craters.

4. Action of different bodies of troops.
   (a) The bombing party are divided as follows.
      (1) The raiding party consisting of 1 Officer and 15 O.R.
      (2) No. 1 blocking party) 4 throwers - 3 carriers 2 Mills
          No. 2 blocking party) Grenade men and one N.C.O. i/c.

   This party will advance as rapidly as possible straight for the S edge of the crater marked L. which is the most northerly crater shown on Brigade Trench Map - area J. They will enter the German trench at the gap caused by the explosion of the most northerly of our new mines.
   The bombing party will bomb along the trench from 41 towards 24, bombing dug outs as they go, as far as they can get in the time allotted.
   No. 1 blocking party will block the German front line trench in a Northerly direction by means of a barrage of bombs thrown from a point in the front line trench marked P.

   No. 2 blocking party will similarly block the C.T. 42 - 43. The N.C.O. will organize his carriers at the junction of these trenches to ensure the supply of bombs to each party.
   (N.B) Each of these carriers is a trained thrower)
   On the signal to withdraw being given the bombing party will withdraw down the trench to 41. On their arrival there the whole will withdraw via S side of crater L to our own lines.

b. The sweeping party will advance in extended order in pairs at 2 yards interval with their right on WINCHESTER ROAD over the craters on to the German front line. Their objective will be the trench from crater F to Pt 41.a. beyond which they will not on any account advance.
   They will thoroughly search the ground in the vicinity of our new craters for wounded or demoralized Germans and will take as many prisoners as possible.
   The O.C. Sweeping party will detail 1 N.C.O. and 4 men to advance via S side of crater L towards point 41 to keep touch with the bombers and to assist them in removing prisoners or wounded.

(e) The Covering party will advance as soon as the sweeping party reaches the near edge of the craters and will take up a position outside but under cover of the craters with their right on WINCHESTER ROAD and their left on crater H. Their duties will be to take back prisoners or wounded and to guide our men during the withdrawal. They will not withdraw themselves until reasonably sure that all our parties are on their way back beyond the craters.

Four Stretcher Bearers without stretchers will accompany the covering party.

The O.C. Assault will be with the covering party.

I suggest that a small party of Mining Experts accompany the sweeping party to search for and destroy enemy mine shafts.

5. The signal for withdrawal will be two long blasts on the whistle. This signal will be given 30 mins after our advance begins – Officers only will give the signal – N.C.Os will repeat. In the event of an Officer i/c of a party being a casualty, the senior N.C.O. may give the signal.

6. Communication. A wire will be run out from our front parapet to crater H and telephone communication established. The signal party will also carry a lamp in case of the wire being cut but no lamp signals will be answered from our front line.

7. Artillery support as arranged – but on the signal that our men are clear an enfilade barrage will be put on German support lines from C C point of salient S of WINCHESTER ROAD to 45. This signal should be some short word such as "FIRE" from Artillery F.O.O. or infantry signal station. If no signal is made then barrage will open automatically at 10-40 P.M.

8. T.M.Batteries to maintain a fire on German front line trench from C C above mentioned to WINCHESTER ROAD till Artillery barrage commences and also on front line to northwards of objective as much as possible.

9. Heavy rifle and M.G. fire to be maintained by troops on both flanks on to German front line throughout the operation or up to 11 P.M. but M.Gs and all riflemen S of WINCHESTER ROAD to have such orders as will ensure their not firing on to the objective.

10. Dress and equipment.
(a) All ranks to wear steel helmets covered with sandbags.
(b) Officers and men to wear distinguishing badge – piece of white material 1" x 3" vertical on back below collar.
(c) All ranks to wear 1914 equipment – belt and pouches only – no haversack or waterbottles – 50 rounds S.A.A. per man and 10 rounds in magazine and every man to carry three bombs.
(d) All pay books, regimental badges and other means of identification except identity discs to be left behind – no documents of any kind to be carried.
(e) Every N.C.O. and man carries a rifle except throwers and stretcher bearers.
(f) Officers of sweeping and covering parties to carry very pistols and ammunition to assist in searching craters.

11. Regimental Aid Posts
Regimental Aid Post will be established in our front line in BAY 40. A lamp will be placed outside and one Sally-Port constructed to admit wounded at BAY 38.

APP A

Report on Raid carried out on 20/3/16.

1. The mines went up at 9.59½. At 10 pm the Bombing party started - followed almost at once by the sweeping party.

The reports of the officers concerned are as follows:-

(a) The Bombing party reached the S. lip of crater L. without opposition but on very heavy going at about 10.5 pm. They entered the German trench just S. of this crater & worked down it. They met 4 Germans who immediately bolted across the open. One of them was wounded by a bomb. They reached the T. junction 41 R. & were counter-attacked with bombs & rifle grenades. A bomb fight followed in which 5 of our bombers were wounded & casualties were certainly inflicted on the enemy, but their extent could not be ascertained, but the bombing Sergt who was wounded early but continued to fight claims to have finished 4 himself & 2 D'Sugan. The bombing officer confirms his story. Our rifle grenade men fired all the time with good effect down main German trench which was well shown up by Very lights. At 10.14 pm the bombing party discovered that their carriers had gone astray & that their bombs were running out - so at 10.16 pm

They withdrew. Meanwhile a small party specially detailed investigated the new crater and looked over the lip & saw 9 dead Germans in the crater. They report that the mine has demolished the Saps 4, 5 & 6 & but has not seriously damaged any of the main trench.
The bombing party including wounded regained our front line at 10.26 pm.

(b) The sweeping party advanced immediately after the bombing party & reached the trench from F to b1 a without opposition, except for some rifle & m.g. fire from the North which wounded 2 men. 7 Germans only were seen unwounded & they were in full flight. One prisoner was captured but could not come back across the crater & had to be killed. The trench above was unoccupied & patrols watched to catch Huns crossing. They report 14 German dead & some six or more were half buried & could not be taken out. A wounded under officer who was not surrendered who killed 3 was found. his coat & the documents & contents are forwarded herewith.

At 10.16 pm the men on the left seeing the bombing withdraw & officer who had been wounded the whole party came back & by about 10.25 pm all were in except

about 20 men under Lieut R.B. PURVES who
remained to make sure no wounded were
left. They returned about 10.3 p.m.

Our casualties were 1 man killed
& 1 officer & 9 other ranks wounded.
All the wounded were brought in but the body
of the dead man had to be left as it was
impossible to carry him over the craters.
The going over the craters was very bad indeed
& all the men who went over sank in over
their knees & returned somewhat exhausted.
I estimate the enemy casualties actually caused
by us to be from 10 to 15 — while at least 20
dead were counted by various parties as
the result of the mine explosion.
It was not possible to get at the bodies to get
means of identification owing to the heat &
gas in the new craters.

(c) A very noticeable feature of the action was
the very effective cooperation of the Trench
Batteries both to N & S of us. They must
have caused many casualties to the enemy

(d) The enemy artillery did not open till about
10.35 p.m. They shelled on flank support &
rear lines quite ineffectively till 11.3 p.m.
at which hour they ceased firing with
4 later shells which caused some incon-
-venience.

4   4

2. Information gained.
   (a) All ranks agree that the trenches in the
       German salient on left that running from
       2a to 41 are unoccupied + derelict
   (1) The bomb... report the bl... at point P
       to be deep well revetted + in good repair.
3. The operation was successful as a whole &
   the men showed no hesitation in leaving
   our parapet or entering the German line.
   The preparation ~~The failure~~ of the bombing party ~~to reach their~~
   ~~objective~~ was entirely due to their carriers
   going astray. They were inadequately found
   all were or less bogged down Point L.
   The bombing party themselves very low heavily
   laden had certainly gone too fast.
   The early retirement of the bombers caused the
   sweeping party to withdraw before the time
   ordered, but as there were no Germans left
   to sweep - they would not have done any
   more damage in the extra 10 minutes.
   In estimation of the ~~failure~~ of the bombers
   I would urge that — they had had very little
   time to organise + practice for this
   particular enterprise + that as long as
   they had bombs they fought with determination
4. Capt R.P.B PURVES very ably organised the
   assault on the short time at his disposal
   + by his personal example kept order in

5.

the with Maxwell & Orr bandaged all our wounded
being brought in.

2nd Lt Ryan led the bombers with great dash
Sergt Cooper the bombing sergt though wounded
in two places early in the affair + ordered
back by his officer - continued to fight &
only came in when the rest of his party
withdrew

W. S. Locker Lt Col.
2/1/16. Comg 9th [Bn] Stafford Regt

War Diary.

SPECIAL ORDER of the DAY
by
Major-General T. Bridges, C.M.G., D.S.O.
Commanding 19th Division.

29/3/16.

The Major-General Commanding has very great pleasure in announcing that, under authority granted by His Majesty the King, the Commander-in-Chief has made the following awards for gallantry in the Field:-

MILITARY CROSS.

Captain P.B. PURVES, 8th (S) Bn. North Staffordshire Regt.
(For commanding and directing, with conspicuous courage and initiative, a successful raid on the German Trenches at THE BIRDCAGE on the night of the 20th March 1916.
When lack of bombs caused the withdrawal of the bombing party earlier than was expected, he at once went forward, organised a rear party, searched the ground and successfully brought in all our wounded - 10 in number.
This Officer's personal example did much to steady the men during a somewhat difficult withdrawal.)

Captain D.W. CROFT, 5th (S) Bn. South Wales Borderers
(Pioneers).
(For conspicuous daring and initiative at the DUCK'S BILL on the 14th March 1916.
After the explosion of an enemy mine, which killed or wounded the majority of the garrison and destroyed the greater part of the work, Captain CROFT went out to render assistance to the garrison and men of his battalion employed there on mining operations.
He then returned and organised a party consisting of 2nd Lieutenant E. St G. YORKE, 18th Bn. Highland Light Infantry, 2nd Lieutenant C.S. LOCHNER, 5th Bn. South Wales Borderers and seven men of his battalion engaged in mining at NEUVE CHAPELLE.
He led his party across to THE DUCK'S BILL, losing two men killed on the way, most of the communication trench having been blown in, necessitating an advance across the open under close rifle fire.
He organised the defence of the remnant of the post and held it until relieved.)

Lieutenant M. ROACH, 255th Tunnelling Company, Royal
Engineers.
(For remarkable courage, determination and devotion to duty whilst mining on the night of the 18th March 1916.
This Officer, hearing the Germans trying to break into one of our mine galleries, lay up single-handed, against the German Timber with a revolver to await them, but was then ordered to blow a small charge against the enemy's timber which he successfully accomplished.
Fifteen minutes later he descended into the mine at great risk to see the result.
After proceeding 50 feet he was overcome by gas and was dragged out by means of a rope round his waist.
He was unconscious for half an hour.
Immediately on coming to, he wished to re-enter our gallery, fearing the enemy would get into it, but was forbidden to do so.
He however refused to leave the trenches that night until the shift was finished.)

P.T.O.

-2-

2nd Lieutenant St D. L. DAVIES, 9th (S) Bn. The Welch Regiment.
(For conspicuous gallantry at FERME DU BOIS on the night of 11/12th March 1916, when he, together with
No. 13985, Corporal T. MAHONEY,
No. 24944, Private E.A. INCE,
No. 18130, " T.T. BRYSON,
No. 14330, " E. JAMES,
9th (S) Bn. The Welch Regiment,
cut a gap through five rows of the German wire in front of the enemy's parapet, to prepare the way for a raiding party, and brought back valuable information regarding the types of wire and system of wiring adopted by the enemy.)

2nd Lieutenant F. St G. YORKE, 18th (S) Bn. Highland Light Infantry.
(For conspicuous gallantry at the DUCK'S Bill on the 14th March, 1916.
After the explosion of a mine which destroyed most of the DUCK'S BILL and communication trench leading to it, 2nd Lieutenant YORKE formed one of a party that crawled out to the BILL under heavy fire to rescue any wounded and reinforce the survivors.
He assisted in organising the defence of the position.)

DISTINGUISHED CONDUCT MEDAL.

No. 14397, Sergeant W. COOPER, 8th (S) Bn. North Staffordshire Regiment.
(For conspicuous courage on the occasion of a successful raid on the German Trenches at THE BIRDCAGE on the night of the 20th March 1916.
Although wounded in two places by a bomb very early in the operations and ordered back by his Officer, he continued to fight and command his party – himself killing four Germans – and only withdrew when the whole party came out.)

No. 17530, Lance Corporal H.W. HARPER, 8th (S) Bn. North Staffordshire Regiment.
(Volunteered to accompany assaulting troops during a raid on the German Trenches at THE BIRDCAGE on night of 20th March 1916.
When the withdrawal commenced he assisted the Officer Commanding the assault to organise a rear party and helped to collect and bring in all our wounded over most difficult ground.
Has on two previous occasions been brought to notice for gallantry under fire.)

No. 13791, Private J. HARRISON, 8th (S) Bn. North Staffordshire Regiment.
(For conspicuous gallantry on the occasion of a bombing raid on the German Trenches at THE BIRDCAGE on the night of the 20th March 1916.
He was thrower to his party and, though wounded by a bomb, he continued to throw until the party finally withdrew.)

No. 5/14712, Lance Corporal P. HIBBERT, 5th (S) Bn. South Wales Borderers (Pioneers).
(For conspicuous courage and coolness under fire at THE DUCK'S BILL on March 14th, 1916.
Lance Corporal HIBBERT formed one of the party under Captain CROFT that went out to THE DUCK'S BILL, under close rifle fire, after that post had been partially destroyed by an enemy mine, and rendered valuable services in assisting to organise the defence and holding the post until relieved.)

P.M. Davies, Lt.-Col.
A.A. & Q.M.G., 19th Division.

SECRET.

ACTION OF TRENCH MORTAR BATTERIES FOR NIGHT 20th/21st MARCH 1916.

Battery	Nature	Position in action	Action	Objective	Approximate Ammunition.
Z.19.	2"	M 24 d 0.4.	Opens fire when the mines, timed for 10 p.m., go up, and fire until 10.45 p.m.	First and second line and M.G.Emplacements M 24 d 3.1. to 4.2 and Sap about 3.5.	50 rounds.
X.19.	1½"	M 24 c 8.1.	-- do --	First and Second line and M.G.emplacements M 24 d 5.1. to M.30.b.8.8.	80 rounds.
Stokes. 57/2.	13 lb.	M 24 c 5.1.	Opens fire at 10.30 p.m. Continue to 10.45 p.m.	C.T. M 30 a 8.5.	90 rounds.
57/1	4 lbs	M 30 a 1.4.	-- do --	M 30 a 4.1.	24 rounds.
No.71	1½". 2 guns	M 29 b 3.0.	Opens fire when the mines go off, timed for 10 p.m.,until 10.45 p.m.	M 30 a 4.0 to 4.1½.	40 rounds.
No.71	1½". 2 guns.	Near DUCK'S BILL	Retaliate vigorously on German Front line opposite DUCK'S BILL for any enemy offensive action in that neighbourhood.		

ACTION OF MACHINE GUNS.

When the mines go up, timed for 10 p.m., long range M.G. fire will be opened on C.Ts. running N. and S.E. from MOULIN DU PIETRE. Front line machine guns will withhold their fire until it is clear that the enemy have manned their parapet or enemy M.Gs. are located in action, but if they have not done so already they will open fire at 10.30 p.m. on enemy parapet from M 30 a 9.5. Northwards and from M 30 a 4.0. Southwards. Fire will be maintained until 10.45 p.m. or later, according to circumstances.

8 N. Staffords vol 10

WAR DIARY / INTELLIGENCE SUMMARY

8th (S) Bn North Staffords Regt. XIX

Army Form C. 2118
Sheet XVII

Place	Date	Hour	Summary of Events and Information	Remarks and references to Appendices
La Gorgue	14/4/16		Marched from La Gorgue to Rue Bailleul; took over billets from 8th Gloucester Regt, who went up into the line.	
Rue Bailleul	11/4/16		Went into trenches; taking over from 8th Gloucesters. 10th Rwar Regt on our left. Enemy very quiet. This I think the first time in trenches during which we suffered no casualties from enemy. Genl. Bridges inspected trenches, & was well satisfied with their cleanliness.	
	15/4/16		Relieved by 8th Gloucesters; went into billets at Rue Bailleul. First day spent in refitting kit. Some to be handed in i.e. 2nd blanket etc; other surplus kit ready to be dumped with other Brigade stuff at Merville.	
	17/4/16		Marched to Merville. Dumped surplus kit on morning of 16th.	
	18/4/16		Marched to old billets at Robecq.	
	20/4/16		Marched to billets at MAMETZ in Brigade. 8th Gloster in Brigade, 10th Worcesters in MARTHES, 10th R War R in WITTERNESSE.	
	21/4/16 to 30/4/16		Started training in 1st Army training area, around Enguingatte; beginning with Platoon & Coy training. Easter Sunday was observed as a holiday. Work started at 8.30 Am & went on till 2 pm with 1 hour break for dinner. Coys arrived back in billets about 3.30 pm. Went on to Bn & BSc training. Lewis gun Detachments, & Bombers received special training.	

W.Y. Foster Lt Col
Cmdg 8th N. Staffords Regt.

WAR DIARY
INTELLIGENCE SUMMARY

8th North Staffordshire Regiment

Vol XIX

8. N Staff C/2118

Place	Date	Hour	Summary of Events and Information	Remarks and references to Appendices
Mametz	1/6/16 to 6/6/16		Continued with Bde & Div training.	
"	7/6/16	2.50pm	Entrained at AIRE Stn. enroute for new area, & detrained at LONGEAU Stn. near AMIENS at about 12 mn. Unloaded horses + vehicles, & cleared the Stn. by 12.45 AM. 8/5/16, marched as Bn. to new billets at VIGNACOURT, about 14 miles N.N.W. reached billets about 7.15 AM. The rest of the Bde. followed during the day. Spent the period here in training, but ground was not very suitable, being practically all cultivation. Divi: sports were held at FLESSELLES, being Div HqR.	
VIGNACOURT	30/5/16 22/6/16	8 Am	Marched as Brigade to training area at ST. RIQUIER, 15 miles N.W. arriving there at 3pm. having had one hours sheaf halt for dinner etc. On this march, Bn. had been one man carried by Field Ambulance. A large draft of 82 arrived on 25th. bringing no that number over strength. Many men were who had been wounded & had left their also sick.	
St RIQUIER	1/6/15		On 30th. May London papers published a despatch by Sir Douglas Haig, in which Bn. were mentioned for good work, this Bn. being one of those mentioned.	

W Lockhurst Lt Col
Cmdg 8 N Staff Regt

Army Form C. 2118
Vol 12
Sheet XIX

E N Staffs

WAR DIARY / INTELLIGENCE SUMMARY
8th (S) Bn. N. Staffd. Regt.
(Erase heading not required.)

Place	Date	Hour	Summary of Events and Information	Remarks and references to Appendices
ST-RIQUIER	1/6/16		Continued training in attack, advancing from assembly trenches, in artillery formation, extending on arrival at captured trench, the edge, & consolidation of position won. The Bde. was frequently reviewed in this manoeuvre, on the last day of training two Bdes., ourselves & 58th practised the exercise together. The Army Commander was present on this occasion. A draft of 13 Officers joined during this period.	
" "	10/6/16 12/6/16		Marched back to same billets at Vignacourt, as a Brigade. At the [?] enemies aircraft.	
VIGNACOURT	13/6/16		Marched as Bn. to Halloy-au-bois, having [?] 2 Pl[?] + 12 men on detachment to Contay & 1 Pl. + 2 B. to Hennencourt.	
Halloy-au-Bois	14/6/16		Marched to between Albert & Dernancourt, & bivouaced. Having arrived, started on supplying working parties for trenches etc.	
	17/6/16		Major Pott joined as 2d in command from 9th R. Welsh Fusiliers. Lieut O'Brien 120 men rejoined.	
Dernancourt	23/6/16	8.30 p.m.	About this time, placed watches on one hour, for Daylight Saving Scheme. Marched from bivouac to billets in Bresle, about 5 miles away. Here got details orders inspecting a big offensive soon to take place, & made all arrangements. Got back most of the Officers given on detachment etc.	
	28/6/16		Completed final arrangements for offensive. Details provided were as given later, together with comments. Marched to Corps Reserve line at Millencourt, where Brigade was formed up. Officer in Reserve to 51st Division is in Millencourt & infantry [?] present for our front.	C Wedgwood [?] Capt. & 2nd in Comd 8th [S] N Staffs Regt

57th Inf.Bde.
19th Div.

8th BATTN. THE NORTH STAFFORDSHIRE REGIMENT.

J U L Y

1 9 1 6

Attached:

Appendices.

Army Form C. 2118
Sheet XX

8th (S) Bn North Stafford Regt.

WAR DIARY / INTELLIGENCE SUMMARY

(Erase heading not required.)

Place	Date	Hour	Summary of Events and Information	Remarks and references to Appendices
Millencourt	1/7/16		Arrived in Corps reserve line, at Tyler's Redoubt at Millencourt, we could see nothing, and began to issue rations, stores etc. Finished by 10 pm 1/7/16.	T.O.
			The "great Offensive", so long looked forward to, began at 7:30 AM; but in Tyler's Redoubt at Millencourt, we could see nothing, and practically nothing. An examination of the "fighting order" as carried by this Bn; (which was that for the whole of the Div) showed that the men in the ranks carried 69 lbs at the very least! The Field Service Manual shows the man in the ranks to carry normally 59 lbs 6½oz. As much kit was discarded in marking up this "light fighting order"; it shows that the present war has pretty increased the impediments that the infantry soldier has to carry.	
			"Light Fighting Order" consisted of the following :-	
			S.A.A. 220 rounds. Bombs 2. Iron Ration 1	
			Cheese 1 lb. Biscuits 2 lbs. Smoke Helmets 2	
			Pick or Shovel 1. Equipment (i.e. Harness-belt, waterbottle, entrenching tool)	
			Besides this, some men carried wire-cutters, others carried flares, & everybody had two sandbags. The Cardigan & waterproof sheet were also carried, an indents in the 69 lbs. Only 2 platoons in each coy carried picks or shovels; Bombers did not carry them.	

WAR DIARY

8th (S) Bn North Stafford Ryt.

INTELLIGENCE SUMMARY

(Erase heading not required.)

Army Form C. 2118
Sheet XXI

Place	Date	Hour	Summary of Events and Information	Remarks and references to Appendices

Such people as Runners (for carrying messages) Scouts, Signallers, L. gun section, & Carrying parties did not carry rifles or shovel, entrenching tool, & had only 50 rds S.A.A.

The Coy. going into action was organized as follows:—
4 platoons to each Coy, (3 lts & 2 Lewis guns with their teams.
Each platoon had two bombing Squads of 5 men each.
Also about 6 men details for wire cutting.
About 4 men were taken from each platoon to form a carrying party.
Which left a platoon roughly 20 men for purely fighting purposes.
But if these 6 men had to be found in the Coy for runners, & each officer had his personal orderly.
The Bn. went into action roughly 790 strong, composed as follows :— (these numbers being the fairly accurate)

H. Coys 640
L. Gunners 56
Bombers 34
Runners 36
Signallers 16
Police 8
                    ———
                    790

Army Form C. 2118
Sheet XXII

WAR DIARY or INTELLIGENCE SUMMARY
8th (S) Bn north Stafford Rgt.
(Erase heading not required.)

Place	Date	Hour	Summary of Events and Information	Remarks and references to Appendices
	2/7/16		The Bn moved from Corps Reserve Line at 7.30 AM 1/7/16, & went to the Intermediate line about Albert, replacing the 56th & 58th Bdes. The whole 17th 57th Bde was in this line with the Bn. The Bde waited here till 5 p.m., then moved up to the TARA USNA line, in front of LA BOISELLE. At 8 p.m., orders were received to advance to the front line, & burst out LA Boiselle, starting the attack at 10.30 P.M. Bn was fallen in, & all the Bombers collected at the hog. Unfortunately no guide was obtainable to guide us up to the front line; till 9.30 p.m. We then started up the one communication trench, which was found to be blocked with wounded, & odd men, chiefly from the TYNESIDE Scottish, & others of the 34th DIV, who had made an attack in the morning. As a result of this, our bombers did not get up till 12 midnight, the 10th Worcesters, who were going to help us in this attack were in the rear of us. The 3 coys that were following, B, a, D, (A being left behind) did not arrive up till 4.30 AM. As a result of this, we did not attack, because it was broad daylight then, & we were went to attack in the dark. This was July reported to 57th Bde, who approved of the action taken. The front line was handed over to 10th R. Warwick Rgt. at 6 AM. & the Bn returned to the Tara Usna by 12 noon.	

WAR DIARY
INTELLIGENCE SUMMARY

Army Form C. 2118
Sheet XXIII

8th (S) Bn North Staffordshire Regt

Place	Date	Hour	Summary of Events and Information	Remarks and references to Appendices

3/7/16

Recd ties 5 pm. 7th were prepared to attack La Boisselle that night, the 8th Bn being on our right, attacking it in the afternoon. Starting off up the C.T. at 11.15 P.M. which was supposed to have been cleared of all troops, but met several stretcher cases which caused delay; finally got whole Bn up by 4 AM. Got the Bn down the front line trench in the following order from right to left; Bn Bombers, 10th Worcesters Bn Bombers, Coy Bombers, D, C, B, A Coys. The last two coys got a bit mixed up coming out of the C.T., some of the 8th Gloucesters got mixed up with us, they were following immediately behind us. Even this time, the whole scheme was too hurried, no time was allowed to explain to the men what was required of them. The first party to go over was one Platoon of D Coy under 2nd Lt. Hunter. They went over about 4.5 AM. & seized the crater in front of the La Boisselle salient, before the Bombers entered. In all 2H bombing parties entered the village before the other troops. The Bn swept up the village & trenches fairly easily at first, up to a point about 3/4 way up. Having reached this far, the bomb supply began to give out, although Bn HQ. men formed a carrying party. By this time, about 100 of the enemy had surrendered. In conjunction with this Bn's attack on the salient of the village, the 10th Worcester Regt, who were

Army Form C. 2118
Sheet XXIV

WAR DIARY
5th (S) Bn North'n Stafford Rgt
INTELLIGENCE SUMMARY
(Erase heading not required.)

Summary of Events and Information

in the front line on our left, having advanced against the North face of the village, joined up with the Bn about 1/3 way up the village. The 8th G'listers Rgt: formed a support in the front line, & 9th Carrying Party. The 10th R. Warwick Rgt: who were on the Worcesters left before the attack, closed down on to the G'listers left. After the Bn had gone about 3/4 way through the village, as before mentioned, the bombs ran short, in spite of a party of G'listers helping in the carrying; so a locally counter-attack by the enemy succeeded in driving us back to a point about 1/4 way up the village. Just when this withdrawal was taking place, at about 6 A.m. the C.O. (Major C. We2 g wooz. D.S.O.) & Major Carruthy (amdg B Coy) were killed by enemy snipers; who were plentiful, & claimed many officers. At this point, many officers had been killed or wounded, & the Bns were mixed up in the line. (It was afterwards found that about 150 men had been fighting in a party well away to the right flank.) two complete Coy's of the Warwicks were sent, one up each flank. These succeeded in turning the enemy flanks, & a combined attack by the whole line drove the enemy back.

Army Form C. 2118
Sheet — XXV

WAR DIARY
8th (S) Bn. North Stafford Regt.
INTELLIGENCE SUMMARY
(Erase heading not required.)

Summary of Events and Information

This was about 8 A.m. By this time, a satisfactory system of carrying parties was working, taking bombs from the Bomb Dump in the front line, to the S end of the village; from that dump up to the firing line. More men also began to come in, from the isolated parties that had been fighting on their own, from the "mopping up" parties, clearing the dug-outs etc behind us; & an advance was made, to well beyond the C.T. leading to Ovillers. A block was established in this trench as we passed. The advance was continued, but a counter-attack on our left unfortunately succeeded in forcing this flank, & as a result of this & more men arriving to re-inforce the enemy, the whole line fell back, & finally consolidated about 1/2 way through the village. This was done approximately at 12 noon, & we held that line till relieved at 6 A.m. 4/7/16. During this fighting, great difficulty was experienced in getting enough Lewis guns to keep the Lewis guns going. An equipment issue just before going into action, A was tried & found useless. The idea was good, but the workmanship was very bad, the stitching & rivetting giving way at the first strain. The men parcels from their equipment were used, answering well for carrying the Lewis guns.

Army Form C. 2118

Sheet XXVI

WAR DIARY
8th Bn Northumberland Fus [?]
INTELLIGENCE SUMMARY
(Erase heading not required.)

Place	Date	Hour	Summary of Events and Information	Remarks and references to Appendices
	4/7/16		As the Germans were emptied, the inclination was first noted to throw them away; but when the difficulty was found in getting up fresh full ones, the problem was solved by having ammunition dumpers at firing places, & the guns being kept in front of [field?] there, brought up again. On relief by 5th Bde, moved back to the old British front line, & stayed there during the day, moving at. It rained heavily during early afternoon, making the trenches a quagmire, & again during the evening. Some of the officers who were left out of action joined HeadQrs, nip having casualties, first before we left Le Boisselle.	

	5/7/16	7.15 AM.	Moved back to the Tara - Usna Line, stayed there half day, moved into billets in Albert in the evening at 8 pm.
			
			Losses in this action Officers 12 Other Ranks 272. Details:-
			
			Killed Major C. Wedgwood, D.S.O. 2nd in Cmd Bn.
			     2/Lt. W. Lawton.
			
			Wounded. Capt. E. I. Colls. Cmdg D Coy.
			     Lt. J. B. Gidley
			     2/Lt. D.e.Q'A Horman
			     2/Lt. C. A. Woodland
			
			     Major J. Carnegy (a/) B Coy.
			     2/Lt. W.G. Fletcher.
			     Lt. W.A. Moir Cmdg C Coy.
			     2/Lt. C. J. Hunter.
			     2/Lt. S. B. Dodman
			     2/Lt. L. V. North.	

WAR DIARY
8th Bn. North Staffs. Regt.
INTELLIGENCE SUMMARY

Army Form. C. 2118
Sheet XXVII

Place	Date	Hour	Summary of Events and Information	Remarks and references to Appendices
Albert	6 & 7th July		Other Ranks:- Killed 28. Wounded 210. Missing 34. Stayed in billets, & started to re-organise the Bn, Major Port from R. Welsh Fusiliers was in Command. A few of the missing men rejoined us, who were missing in the beginning; they having been cut off, joined other Bns.	
"	8/7/16	1 p.m.	Received orders to join 56th Bde in firing line. Three Coys went up to reconnoitre, taking one Officer per Coy with him. Bn marched off from billets at 8.30 pm & got guides at the Bn on Bapaume road at about 10 pm. As the Bn we were relieving (13th R. Fusiliers) had just any advanced 600 yds; the guides were a bit uncertain as to the Coy's whereabouts. Coys were finally got together at Bn HQ. I went up to the Franklin trench positions. To add to the general discomfort, the enemy were shelling all the front line that we passed over pretty hotly. On arrival in the front line, the 11th R. War. Regt. should have been in position on our right, but they were not. Their HQ about 11.30 pm not knowing the Royal Irish Rifles on our left had advanced beyond their objectives, were held a hundred well within our trench & refused to come back. Hence our left & their right were not touching. Finally both the frontier with B. C. D Coys in firing line, & A in support. R. Guns with this coys, Bn Bombers in reserve near Bn H.Q. Supporting us were 7th S. Lancs.	

Army Form C. 2118
Sheet XXVII

WAR DIARY
8th Bn. North Stafford Regt.
INTELLIGENCE SUMMARY
(Erase heading not required.)

Instructions regarding War Diaries and Intelligence Summaries are contained in F.S. Regs., Part II. and the Staff Manual respectively. Title Pages will be prepared in manuscript.

Place	Date	Hour	Summary of Events and Information	Remarks and references to Appendices
Q/7/16	9/7/16		The Bys were firmly in position by 5.30 A.m. was heavily shelled at 9.30 A.m & it stopped about 11.30 A.m. Shells about 12.30 P.m. stopped at 4 P.m. About this time enemy made two bombing attacks, one on our left where gap existed, & one on our right flank. Both were driven back, broken for our relief reached us very late, at 10.30 P.m. Got pushed off to the 13th Rifle Brigade, & relief was complete at 3.30 P.m. Bn HQ being the last to go out, left the front line & got to the Tara Usna line at 5 P.m. 10th.	App. I Remarks by 57th Brigade. App. II. Letters from G.O.C 8 Bn.
	10/7/16		Bn marched from Albert, where it collected, to bivouac in Millencourt, getting in about 8 A.m. Casualties this tour:- Officers Killed 2/Lt C.T. Eazdy 2/Lt E.B. Thorp. Wounded Capt. F.A.S. Gibson. Wounded Capt. G.R. Ford. Other Ranks. Killed 8. Wounded 45. Missing 3. Missing, since reported killed	
Millencourt	11/7/16 to 19/7/16		Began to re-organise the Bn, & practise Bombing Squads, the Lewis gun teams etc. Receiving drafts as follows:- 2/Lt J.R. Campion - Coles 4th H.O.R. N. Staffords. 81. O.R. Dublin Fusiliers. 49. O.R. Middlesex Regt. 2/Lt E.C. Hale.	
	20/7/16		Marched at night to Bivouac by Becourt Wood.	
	21/7/16		Marched up to the line via Fricourt, guiding into the line by Bazentin-le-Petit, the country of the Windmill. This relief was done through a	

WAR DIARY INTELLIGENCE SUMMARY

8th (S) Bn North Staffordshire Regt.

Army Form C. 2118
Sheet XXIX

Place	Date	Hour	Summary of Events and Information	Remarks and references to Appendices
	23/7/16 to 24/7/16		Very heavy enemy barrage, & about 30 men were lost for the time being in one Coy which got caught. The relief was a bit muddled, the guides having to take Coy's across country owing to the barrage. Finally we got into position, the 10th Worcesters being on our right front, & in front of us also, the point to the 2nd Worcesters on their right, & we joined with 56th Bde on our left, about 200 yds East of Bazentin-le-Petit village. Were heavily shelled during our tour of the line this time, especially the Bn. H.Q. in the Chalk Pit, & the bit of trench by it; also the Windmill. The shelling was almost continuous, but was especially heavy on the night of 23-24th, when the 56th Bde, with 10th R. Warwicks & 8th Gloucesters of this Bde attacked the enemy intermediate line on our front. The attack was not a success with our two Bns., the enemy barrage Guns being still intact. Enemy put up a heavy barrage with 5.9", 4.2" & lighter guns from about 2 p.m. to 5 to kill 9 our line till 5 AM. This morning 24th we endeavoured to establish a strong point about 100 yds N.E. of the Windmill, vacating the line 50 yds either side of it, to the Windmill was a mark for the enemy guns.	

Army Form C. 2118

Sheet XXX

WAR DIARY
1st (9) Bn North Staffs Regt
INTELLIGENCE SUMMARY
(Erase heading not required.)

752
SB

Place	Date	Hour	Summary of Events and Information	Remarks and references to Appendices
	28/7/16 to 31/7/16		Placed the men in position, but got one team of L.G. gunners & a squad of Bombers with them buried by a shell, but re-established them. Were relieved by 5.8th Batt on the evening of 31st. Orders for the attack that was made were very late in arriving. We were unable to carry out our part, i.e. to send one platoon with 10th Worcesters, for the others arrived after the Worcesters had hung from their position, owing to the way to the attack. However, we sent two cox's to # accompany the second trenches held by the G to the two Worcesters, & got orders to withdraw them later. Were relieved by 5.8th Batt evening of 30th. Got relief done before dark, so escaped the nightly shelling. Marched back to bivouac in Becourt Wood. Went into the line again, the same place as before, twice in reserve to the 2nd; held the King's Own & Cheshire Rgt from 5.8th Batt next to us, to attack the intermediate line of the enemy. This attack succeeded on the right & right centre, the King's Own & ½ 10th R.W. arriving. 6 the left it failed from the reoccurance as before. Dy in giving the rig. up with the keep of the S.W.B. (Pioneers). Were relieving on the night of 31/7/16 - 1/8/16, & got out before dark again. The whole Div came out this time.	

Army Form C. 2118

Sheet XXVI

WAR DIARY

8th (9) Bn. North or Stafford Regt

INTELLIGENCE SUMMARY

(Erase heading not required.)

753a

We had the same form as the last one.
Casualties in the period 21st – 27th. 6 Officers:–
Major G.S. Crawford (from 5th Sw. B) wounded 2Lt Lt. Masters   wounded
2Lt R.G. Gough   "   2Lt R.F. Potter   did y wound
  "   W. Shaw   "   2Lt F.H. Phillips wounded
  "   Cpt. Booth   "   2Lt h.g. Baker   —
  "   W.H.F. Barklam   "   2Lt Jm Campion-Cole —
                                        missing 2H.

O.R. Killed 18.   Wounded 89.

Casualties in the period 28th – 31st. Officers:–
2Lt A.g. Saunders   Killed   2Lt W.T. Lerway Wounded
  "   J. Morton   Wounded   2Lt E.C. Hale   —
  "   G.D. Bolton   " at Duty.

O.R. Killed 9.   Wounded 36   missing 9.

O.C. Stanthorpe
Capt. a/t.
8 N. Stafford Regt

1875 Wt. W593/826 1,000,000 4/15 J.B.C. & A. A.D.S.S./Forms/C. 2118.

A P P E N D I C E S .

(671)

19 Div⟨ision⟩ G. 758.

The attached letter to O.C.
57 B⟨rigad⟩e to forward please.
Will you please give it
to the undermentioned officer
personal.

J. Busby

57th Brigade

Forward.

19th Div⟨ision⟩
13.7.16. To 8' B⟨attalio⟩n. Staff. R.
14.7.16. Tomardai

[stamp: HEADQUARTERS 56th INFANTRY BRIGADE — No. Bm 779 C. — Date 11/7/16]

G.O.C.
57th Brigade

759E
CB

During the recent operations near LA BOISELLE the 8th Bn North Staffordshire Regt belonging to your Brigade came under my command. This battalion took over the front line trenches from the 13th Bn Royal Fusiliers on the night of the 8th-9th July & remained in possession for 24 hours. During this period they consolidated the trenches & were subjected to a very heavy hostile shell fire. On the afternoon of the 9th inst the Battalion repelled two bombing attacks made by the enemy.

I deplore the casualties incurred which, under the above circumstances, were inevitable. The Battalion displayed great coolness & steadiness throughout.

11.7.16 -

 L. Rowley, B. Genl
Comdg 56th Inf Brigade

The following points were noticed during the fighting of the 57th Brigade at LA BOISSELLE, from the 2nd to the night 3th/4th July.

The case was exceptional, and as far as one knows outside the experience of any member of the Brigade. The fighting devolved into a struggle for the possession of a strong point, built in and round a small village, the near or Western edge of which was covered by a series of defensive craters. In the centre of the village was an inner strong point or keep, the whole being under-mined with subterranean passages connecting up mine heads and deep dug-outs, with numerous lateral and longitudinal communication trenches.

Once the outer edges of the village had been reached, further progress could only be made by means of bombing parties of varying sizes who necessarily got much separated and at times quite cut off from all communication with their own, so called supports. These supports themselves became involved in small affrays, often some way behind their own lines.

In this style of fighting it was found that nearly all the Regimental Bombers of all four battalions were drawn early into the battle and after an hour or two's fighting were quite worn out and could advance no more. Every effort was made to relieve these men by any other bombers who could be found, and were thus able to force an advance for a short distance. These in turn required relieving and this was found to be a very difficult matter. The various parties became quite independent, each fighting for its own ends, and most difficult to control. It is believed that many of our Officer casualties resulted from their endeavouring to make the operations more cohesive, & for all to work for one end.

There was dozens of dug-outs or cellars, or at any rate entrances, each of which required to be dealt with separately, necessitating an abnormal number of bombs. In connection with this it is certain that there was quite an unnecessary expenditure of bombs, which it would always be hard to regulate, more especially with troops who are really participating in their first aggressive battle.

With a view to curtailing this wastage, it is proposed that actual bombers should not carry quite so many bombs on their persons but that the bombing party should be increased by a carrier or if necessary two, thereby relieving the throwers from some of the great weight they have to carry and thus keeping them fresher for a longer period.

Though the parties were told off for mopping up purposes, these found themselves drawn into the chief engagement. In the case of a Brigade attack on such a point, two battalions make the assault, one battalion entire should be told off as garrison of the post under its C.O. as O.C. and do nothing else but mop up, and consolidate. This would leave one battalion as support, or in Brigade Reserve, this might limit the extent of the advance, but undoubtedly would tend to make that particular point good with considerably less loss of life and chance of the first advance being cut off.

The matter of communication, as always, was a matter of great necessity and difficulty, especially in such labyrinth of trenches and craters, while communication trenches are full of reinforcing troops or of dead and wounded, and where runners are so apt to lose themselves. Telephone wires when laid seldom lasted more than a few minutes in advance of Brigade H.Q. and all messages had to be sent by runners from the front to the Advanced Report Centre and thence by the same means to Brigade H.Q.

(2)

On this occasion there was only one communication trench between the USNA TARA line and the point of our old trench from which the assault was made, by which all traffic up and down had to go. Another Communication Trench was really essential.

As regards Stokes Mortars, it was found :-

(1) That to use them effectively during an assault was practically impossible, but as soon as some footing had been gained they were most useful to maintain the position, and also to prepare the way for a fresh advance.

(2) The easiest way of carrying shells is in sandbags slung over the shoulder.

(3) Some means of communication is necessary between the observer and his gun, probably a shutter would be the best as a telephone wire would last no time.

(4) Two picks and two shovels per mortar are necessary for making emplacements.

(5) Shoulder Jackets as supplied to Machine Gunners would be of great assistance in carrying mortars and elevating stands.

Both the Machine Gun Company and the Trench Mortar Battery found great difficulty in discovering whether a certain portion or line of trench had been taken or not, and it is suggested that the old pattern artillery screens might be usefully employed for this purpose.

The system of getting bombs, Stokes mortar shells, S.A.A., water and rations up to the front line which it is proposed to employ in future, and which was employed for conveying everything except rations on this occasion is as follows :-

A Brigade Carrying Party carries from the Divnl Dump to an advanced dump, which in this case was our old front line trench, opposite LA BOISSELLE, and from this advanced dump units made their own arrangements to supply their front line, either by forming a forward dump at selected places close behind the front line from which the front line supplied themselves, or else carried straight from the advanced dump to the front line. The first alternative is considered the best as it prevents wastage of stores. It is considered important that all carriers should wear some distinctive badge and thus prevent leakage to the rear of shirkers. From the Divisional Dump to the advanced dump, this is not so important as these parties are properly organised and under an officer, but in advance of the advanced dump the distinctive mark is considered most important.

To summarize :-

(1) The relay system of supply was found to work very satisfactory.

(2) The throwers were too heavily laden performed, and having so many bombs immediately at hand threw them indiscriminately.

(3) Trench Mortars are invaluable once a footing in the enemy's line has been gained, but are of little use in the actual assault.

(4) The covering fire from Machine guns proved very effective and efficient.

(5) Machine guns and trench mortars found it very difficult to discover the exact position of our most forward parties.

(6) Bombing parties must be relieved frequently, they advance a certain distance, and then being tired and worn out, they block and remain stationary throwing a large number of bombs unnecessarily.

(7) In the case of a village, wood or other strong point, one unit should be given the definite task of clearing up, leaving the rest of the Brigade free to advance.

(8) Wireless to be of any use, as far as the Brigade is concerned, should be used from Battalion H.Q. to Brigade H.Q., it is between these points that the telephone wires are so frequently cut. Every Battalion H.Q. should be allowed to use the code.

(9) In addition to the petrol cans supplied by dumps, 50 cans per water cart could be carried in a crate on the cart and would prove most useful.

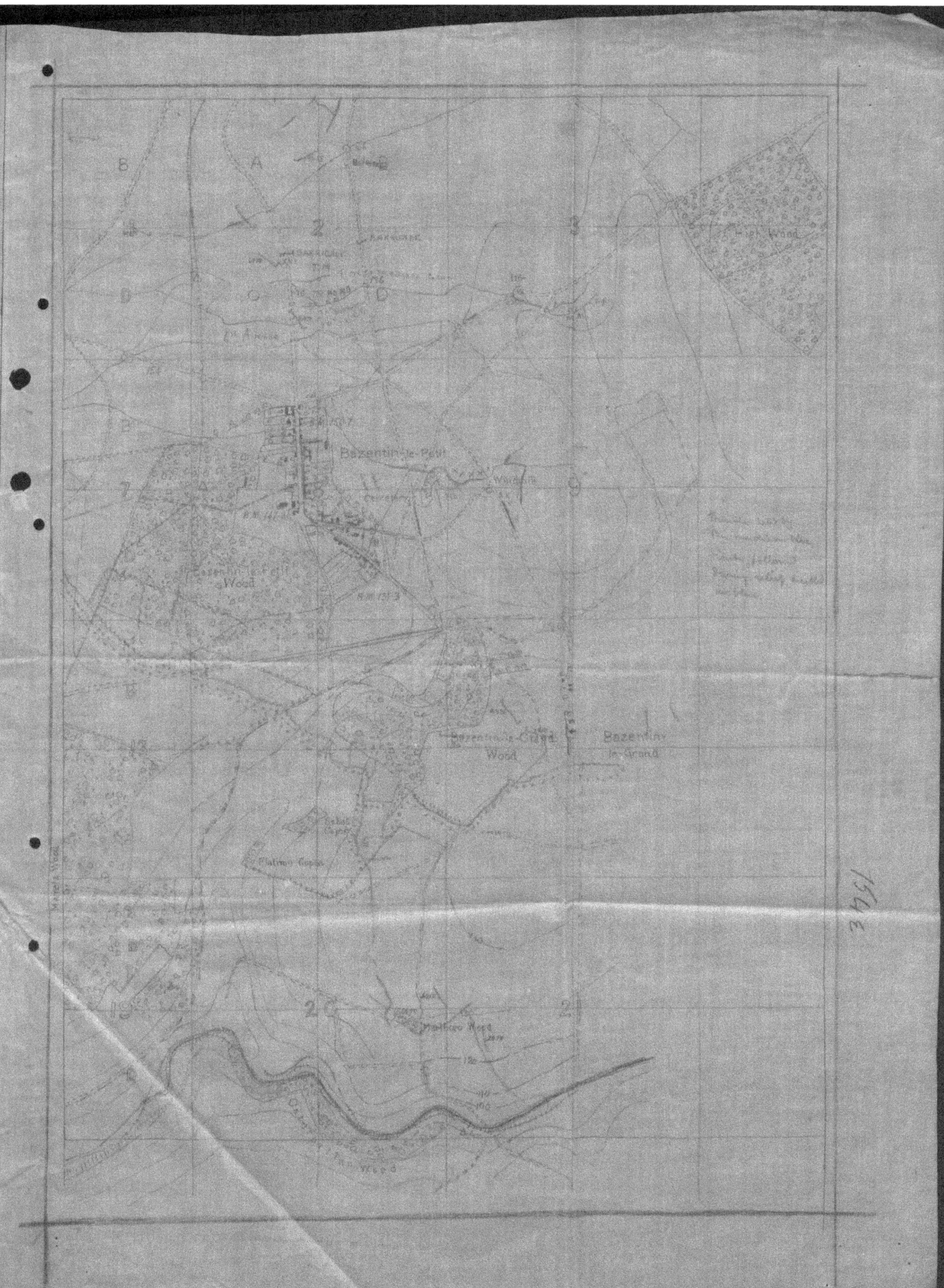

57th Brigade.
19th Division.

1/8th BATTALION

NORTH STAFFORD REGIMENT

AUGUST 1 9 1 6

Army Form C. 2118

WAR DIARY
INTELLIGENCE SUMMARY

8th (S) Bn North. on Stafford Ryt.

Vol 14

Place	Date	Hour	Summary of Events and Information	Remarks and references to Appendices
BECOURT WOOD	31/7/16		Marched to BRESLE, billeting there. Began to refit & re-organise the Bn. Had a special Parade for the Corps Commander, the Bde, 5th S.W.B. (Pioneers) & 82nd Field Coy R.E. being present. Corps Commander thanked Bns for their work & gave a farewell speech on the Bde leaving the Corps.	
BRESLE	3/8/16		Bn marched to MERICOURT, & entrained, the Transport having left the day before, to go by route-march to new billets. Bn detrained at LONGPRE, & marched to L'ETOILE, billeting there. The rest of the Bde was billeted in the villages round about.	
L'ETOILE	6/8/16		Marched to LONGPRE, & entrained again, with Transport, & detrained at BAILLEUL, marched to bivouac on the side of KEMMEL HILL.	
	7/8/16		Went in the morning to the trenches, & relieved 4th Northumberland Fus. that evening. 10th R. War. R. on our left, Ulster Div: on our right. Transport was far away to our right front.	
	10/8/16		Were relieved by 8th Gloucester Ryt: & went into Bde Reserve.	
	14/8/16		Relieved the Gloucesters in the trenches.	
	18/8/16		The usual relief took place, Bn went to Div: Reserve in Dranoutre.	

Army Form C. 2118

Sheet XXXIII

WAR DIARY
87 (3) Bn North or S Stafford Reg.
INTELLIGENCE SUMMARY
(Erase heading not required.)

Instructions regarding War Diaries and Intelligence Summaries are contained in F.S. Regs., Part II. and the Staff Manual respectively. Title Pages will be prepared in manuscript.

Place	Date	Hour	Summary of Events and Information	Remarks and references to Appendices
22/8/16			The usual relief took place. 3 days in 5 days. Came in, 3 coys with us, for instruction.	
	24/8/16		Usual relief, went into Bde Reserve.	
	26/8/16		Bn assisted in carrying up gas cylinders to the front line, as we were to do a raid, + gas was to be liberated.	
	29/8/16		C.O. went to trenches, in case wind was suitable for liberation of Gas, but it was not suitable.	
	31/8/16		Went to the trenches in usual relief.	

J.R. Paviot Lieut Col.

WAR DIARY or INTELLIGENCE SUMMARY

Army Form C. 2118

Vol 15 Sheet XXXIV

1st/(5) Bn. Staffordshire Regt.

Place	Date	Hour	Summary of Events and Information	Remarks and references to Appendices
Trenches	3/9/16		Made a raid this night on the enemy trenches, but were unsuccessful; chiefly owing to the leading officer & H.F. Day being killed at the very beginning when the party were entering the enemy trench.	
	4/9/16		Relieved this evening by Canadians, & billets in Dranoutre.	D
DRANOUTRE	6/9/16		Moved to new area at Ploegsteert, & billets at Le ROMARIN, whole Brigade had moved; Taken over a section of trenches in Ploegsteert Wood, & to the north of it.	D
Le ROMARIN	12/9/16		Relieved 5th Gloucester Regt in the line, 5th R.B. on right, 10th R. Worcesters on left.	D
Trenches	16/9/16		Relieved by 5th Gloucester Regt, went into Bde reserve, at Red Lodge.	D
Red Lodge	20/9/16		Bn was relieved by 1st South Staffordshire Regt; & marched to billets in METEREN	D
	21/9/16		Bn marched & billeted in PRADELLES, near Hazebrouck, with the other Bns of the Brigade in villages close by.	D
	27/9/16		Inspection of the Brigade by the Army Commander.	D

H.S. Osborne Major
Cmdg 1/5th N. Staffs Regt.

Army Form C. 2118

57/19 Vol 16

WAR DIARY / INTELLIGENCE SUMMARY

8th (S) Bn North Stafford Regt

Place	Date	Hour	Summary of Events and Information	Remarks and references to Appendices
PRADELLES	3/10/16		Inspection of 8th Bn & 5th (S) Bn South Wales Borderers by H.M. King of the Belgians. Guard of Honor. A cyclist escort in the South of 24th H.P. BUNCE & Cpl. Hughes, & wounded one private. Tpr. Left billets, marched to BAILLEUL WEST STN, & entrained for new area. Tpr left at 1 A.M. 8th Bn left at 3.30 A.M. Detrained at DOULLENS, & marched about 7 miles into billets in BOIS de WARNIMONT, about 7 miles to HEBUTE THEIVRES. Rest of Brigade being billeted in villages near by.	
"	5/10/16			
"	6/10/16			
THEIVRES	7/10/16		Marched at 2 P.M. to huts in BOIS de WARIMONT, all from Bns, Bde H.Q. being in ST LEDGER.	
BOIS de WARIMONT	9/10/16		Parties went up to HEBUTERNE, about 7 miles, to inspect that part of a possible offensive from this front. One private was killed by shell fire on 9/10/16 with these parties. Practice attacks in Artillery formation. B/col. C.L. Anderson joins Bn.	
"	10/10/16			
"	17/10/16		Marched as a Brigade across country to WARLOY, & billets there.	
WARLOY	20/10/16		Marched as Brigade to ALBERT BRICKFIELDS, & bivouacs there.	
"	27/10/16		The C.O. & Coy commanders going into action went ahead of Bn to the trenches, Bn marched to trenches, having seen of former fights at La BOISSELLE, to STUFF REDOUBT & Regina Trench, capturing the day before. 5th L. Bn was on our left, 10th Worcester Regt. on our right. Stayed in trenches two days, & had heavy casualties from shell fire, 78 O.R. in all. Had bad weather, & a very trying time returning after relief by 2nd 8th Gloucesters Regt. Bn getting in	

WAR DIARY or INTELLIGENCE SUMMARY

Army Form C. 2118

Place	Date	Hour	Summary of Events and Information	Remarks and references to Appendices
Trenches.	24th to 30th		During the early hours of the morning of Sept. 2nd & 4th. We in the old German front line; aeroplanes in dug-outs with a 60 lb. battery & 18 pr. battery firing over the trench; hair shaves themselves a bit, but the weather was very uncertain.	
	30/10/16 to 31/10/16.		Went up to front line in relief of 5/8th Bn. Took over same line as before; had some heavy rain; trenches filled with water; the sides falling in, where holes had been dug in the parados & parapet. Mud was up to over thighs, & became very sticky. 8th G Loucester Regt started to relieve us at 11.45 pm. Relief was completed by 6.20 pm; then only because we went over the open as soon as it got dark. Trench ways had been laid over the open part of the way back, which helped greatly. Went back to the same dug-outs as before. The Co. Price F.W. Parish went away as a casualty the afternoon of 1/11/16, day of relief. Other Casualties 1 O.R. killed, 21 wounded, 5 missing.	

(signature)
Capt 8th N Stafford Rt
(signature)

WAR DIARY
or
INTELLIGENCE SUMMARY

Army Form C. 2118

Place	Date	Hour	Summary of Events and Information	Remarks and references to Appendices
Trenches	24th to 30th		During the early hours of the morning of 29th, 2 H.E. Shells in the old German front line, aeroplanes in day-outs, with a 60 lb. battery & 18 p battery firing over the trench; hour shows themselves a bit, but the weather was very miserable.	
	30/10/16 31/10/16		Went up to front line in relief of 58th 13 Bde. Took over same line as before; had some heavy rain, & trenches filled with water; the side is falling in, where holes had been dug in the parados & parapet. Hun was up to own flights, & became very shelly. 8th Gloucester Rgt. started to relieve us at 11:45 pm. Relief was completed by 6.20 pm; then only because we went over the open as soon as it got dark. Trench boards had been laid over the open part of the way back, which helped greatly. Went back to the same day-outs as before. The Co. Pryce F.W. Parish went away as a casualty the afternoon of 1/11/16, day of relief. 6th the Caanarton, 1 O.R. killed, 21 wounded, 5 missing.	
	1/11/16			

Cecil 8th N. Staffordsh

Army Form C. 2118

WAR DIARY
or
8th (S) B" North Stafford's Regt
INTELLIGENCE SUMMARY

(Erase heading not required.)

Instructions regarding War Diaries and Intelligence Summaries are contained in F.S. Regs., Part II. and the Staff Manual respectively. Title Pages will be prepared in manuscript.

Place	Date	Hour	Summary of Events and Information	Remarks and references to Appendices
TRENCHES	1-11-16	11.45 a.m	The B" being relieved by 8th Gloucester Regt. Relief completed by 6.20 P.M and then only because we went over the open as soon as it was dark. Trench had been laid in the open part of the way back which helped greatly. Went back to DANUBE TRENCH to rest. The C.O. Lt Col F.W. Parish went astray as a casualty on the afternoon. Casualties 1 O.R. 36 killed, 21 Wounded, 5 Missing.	
DANUBE Trench	2-11-16	2 P.M	Left DANUBE Trench and proceeded to Rest Billets nr Crucifix Corner arrived there 3.30 P.M.	
CRUCIFIX Corner nr AVELUY	3-11-16		In reserve billets carried out general training.	
- " -	4-11-16		Training carried on throughout the day.	
- " -	5-11-16		General training continued as on 3rd & 4th	
- " -	6-11-16		General training of Batt." and lecture by C.O. on discipline	
- " -	7-11-16		Training carried out as on other days.	
- " -	8-11-16	2 P.M	B" paraded in fighting order and marched to Front line same Trench as before and relieved Y + B" East Lanc Regt	
Trenches	9-11-16		Continual work carried out repairing parapets and paradoes, draining trench.	
- " -	10-11-16		Work of repairing and draining carried on under moderate Artillery fire.	
- " -	11-11-16		Still in front line work carried on as on the 10th	
- " -	12-11-16		B." relieved at 10 P.M and marched back to MARLBOROUGH HUTS. AVELUY arrived there about 12 M.N.	
MARLBOROUGH HUTS	13-11-16		General cleaning up and training carried on during the morning. Lecture given by C.O. to all officers on proposed operations	
- " -	14-11-16		General training during the morning. Platoon commanders lectures their platoons on operations about to take place.	
- " -	15-11-16		Training of companies carried on under Company Commanders	
- " -	16-11-16		General training of coys during the morning. B" paraded at 3 P.M. to proceed to front line. This order was cancelled before marching off. All returned to huts. Conference of all officers at 7 P.m provided over by the Brigadier	

WAR DIARY

8(S) Batt or **North Staffords Regt** continued

INTELLIGENCE SUMMARY

Army Form C. 2118

Vol 12

Place	Date	Hour	Summary of Events and Information	Remarks and references to Appendices
MARLBOROUGH HUTS.	17.11.16		Snowing carried on during the morning, bombs, S.A.A. Rockets &c issued out to 13th Companies of Officers at 3.02 on operations to be carried out next morning. 13th marched off 3 p.m. to STUFF REDOUBT and remained there until 3.A.M. 18.11.16	
REGINA Trench	18.11.16		Soup and Rum served out to 13th previous to forming up to attack DESIRE Trench the O.B.1. Snowy fell during the night and it was very cold. Exactly at 6.10 A.M. the Artillery Barrage opened and the first wave moved off hugging quite close to the Barrage. After communication of operations all Touch seemed to have been lost with the Batt. The attack having failed the survivors made their way as best they could to the O.B.1. from where the attack started from in the morning. One officer 2 Lieut A. Sidham left in temporary command of 13th. then left. Casualties 1 4 Officers, 319 O.R. Capt. G.E. Jarvis 16 killed Lieut. Col. B.L. Anderson Missing Believed Killed, 11 Other Capt. A.E. Standbridge Dead Lieut. T.S. Mackie " Capt (Temp.Capt) R. Naughting " 2 Lieut G. H. Howells " 2 Lieut. E.V. Turner — " — Lieut J.W. Duffy 2 Lieut A.W. Duffy " — S. J. Loudon " — H.R. Gregorie " — E.B. Bolton " Lieut H. Adams Missing — " W. D. Henderson — " — P.B. Hughes — " — E. Campbell — " — J.E. Good 15 wounded — " N.F. Cook — "	
"	19.11.16		Still holding Front Trench very little hostile artillery but plenty of sniping going on. 13th relieved at 10 PM and returned to Marlborough Huts under the Command of Lieut E.G. Smith who had gone to front line and taken over temporary command earlier in the day. Total number returned who had taken part in the attack were 1 Officer 171 O.R.	
MARLBOROUGH HUTS.	20.11.16		Cleaning up and making up deficiencies.	
"	21.11.16		Same as for 20th	
"	22.11.16		Marched to WARLOY and moved off 7-50 A.M. Major H. W. Rakugne 10 R.W. Rgt assumed Temporary command of the 13th	
WARLOY.	23.11.16		General training and cleaning of billets.	
"	24.11.16		B" moved off at 6-43 Am en route to HERRISART.	
HERRISART.	25.11.16		Marched to FIEFFES. arrived 12.15 P.M.	
FIEFFES.	26.11.16		B" moved off 10-35A.M. arrived FIEFFES 5.15 P.M.	
ST. OUEN.	27.11.16		B" moved to new billets at ST OUEN at 10 Rkm arrived nearly the whole time, arrived ST OUEN 1.15 P.M.	
ST. OUEN	28.11.16 7-35A		Sunday Inspection of Billets.	
LONGUEVILL.	29.11.16 30.11.16		Moved to LONGUEVILLETTE arrived at LONGUEVILLETTE Church 1 PM. good billets but no sanitation. General cleaning and arranging Rifle and Bombing Ranges	

H. Darwin Major
Commanding 8 B" North Staffords Regiment

WAR DIARY
8th (S) B.n North Staffordshire Regt.
INTELLIGENCE SUMMARY

Army Form C. 2118

Vol 18

Place	Date	Hour	Summary of Events and Information	Remarks and references to Appendices
LONGUEVILL ETTE.	1-12-16		B.n in rest billets. General Training carried out.	JL
"	2-12-16		Training. 10. O.R.s joined 13th Bombing class. Capt Tichborne C.F. rejoined B.n off leave.	JL
"	3-"-"		Sunday.	JL
"	4-"-"		General Training carried out. 2nd Lt A.H. Sillem and 19. O.R.s joined Divisional Lewis Gun Class. Capt B.M. Fletcher rejoined from leave.	JL
"	5-"-"		General Training. A draft of 194. O.R.s joined B.n 26 Officers. Lieut + Q.M. + Crewe proceeded on leave to England.	JL
"	6-"-"		10. O.R.s rejoined from B.n Bombing Class. 12 O.R.s joined 13th Bombing Class.	JL
"	7-"-"		General Training + constructing Rifle Range + Bombing Ground.	JL
"	8-"-"		Noon. 6th Draft of 9. O.R.s joined 13th	JL
"	9-"-"		Training. 2 Lt Boulton and 2. O.R.s joined Divisional, Junior Officers + N.C.O. School of Instruction. Capt D.W. Fletcher admitted to Hospital.	JL
"	10-"-"		Training carried on. Two Officers joined B.n Major J.C.C. Thomas (2nd In Command), and Major D. Shakespeare.	JL
"	11-"-"		Sunday. One O.R. joined Class of instruction for Musketry Instructor at CAMIERS. 1.O.R joined Divr G.A.S School	JL
"	12-"-"		10. O.R. joined 13th from 13th Bombing Class.	JL
"	13-"-"		General Training 6. O.R.s joined course of instruction in Lewis Gun at ETAPLES. 8.O.R.s joined 13th Bombing Class.	JL
"	14-"-"		3. O.R.s joined Divisional Bombing Class.	JL
"	15-"-"	9-30AM	Training carries on. Draft of 46 joined 13th	JL
"			General Training carried out. Three Officers joined 13th Capt G.F.H. Bill. Lieut. G.P Smith + R.n D.S. Hancock also Lt. O.B.s Training carried out. 5 instructions of 13th by Corps Commander B.n Goo M.O. formed up in mass and afterwards marched past in fours. B.n was by week. Having provided working Party of 2 Officers + 150. O.R.s Very wet morning but about afternoon first before going on parade. One O.R joined Divisional G.A.S School. 8. O.R.s rejoined from Brigade Bombing Class Major J.T.E. + G.S. Uldan joined 13th	JL
"	16-"-"		Training Carried on. 2nd Lieut A.H Sillem and 18 O.R.s rejoined from Divisional Lewis Gun School.	JL
"	17-"-"		Sunday. 2nd Lieut D.C. Rogers + 16. O.R.s joined Divisional Lewis Gun School. Draft of 167. O.R.s joined 13th	JL
"	18-"-"		General Training.	JL
"	19-"-"		Training Draft of 56 Officers joined 13th Lieut H.Meredith Pruitt P.A. Burridge, H.C. Maule, J.L. Brooks + F Clarke. 6. O.R.s rejoined from Lewis Gun School CAMIERS.	JL

WAR DIARY
8(S) Bn North Staffordshire Regt.
INTELLIGENCE SUMMARY

Army Form C. 2118

Place	Date	Hour	Summary of Events and Information	Remarks and references to Appendices
LONGUEVILLE TTE.	20/12/16		General Training Carried out. 1 OR rejoined from Div. Gas School. 1 OR Joined Div Gas School.	JM
"	21-12-16		Training Carried on.	OK
"	22-"		Training Carried out.	JM
"	23-"		Training continued	
"	24-"		Sunday Div class rejoined B: for X.MAS.	JM
"	25-"		Christmas day. Dinners served to men in canteen and school. Tugowar Hunt and football match officers v sergts in the afternoon. Very wet practically all the day. Concert in the canteen in the evening. All officers dined together.	JM
"	26-"		Divisional class rejoined against the School. Capt G P Smith and 1 OR joined Russ Gun School LETOUQUET. General Training carried on.	JM
"	27-"		Training carried on. 1 OR joined Div School for Training as musketry Instructor.	JM
"	28-"		Training Carried on.	JM
"	29-"		Training. All officers joined Brigade Bombing class. Three officers and 9 OR joined B'n 2/Lt O.F.W. Greeves, RT Cottrill and R.W. OWEN. Lieut Col. H.W DAKEYNE. and Major G Sullivan proceeded on leave to England.	JM
"	30-"		Training carried on practice new formation of attack. 4 OR joined Divisional Bombing School	JM
"	31-"		Sunday. all officers completed Brigade Bombing class. Lieut Col. A. CARTON De WIART. V.C. D.S.O. B' 8/Loo Regt. assumed temporary command of B': Capt John M.O. proceeded on leave to England Capt in place of Capt John.	JM

31-12-16

R Milnes Mj n/Lieut Col
Comdg 8 B/North Staffordshire Regt.

19 8th N. Staffords
       Vol. 8

Army Form C. 2118

WAR DIARY
or
INTELLIGENCE SUMMARY
(Erase heading not required.)

8 N Staffords Regt

Instructions regarding War Diaries and Intelligence Summaries are contained in F.S. Regs., Part II and the Staff Manual respectively. Title Pages will be prepared in manuscript.

Place	Date	Hour	Summary of Events and Information	Remarks and references to Appendices
LONGUEVILLETTE	1-1-17	—	General Training carried on. Captain Strinbridge returned off leave. 1 O.R. joined Divisional Gas Course.	
"	2-1-17		General Training. 2nd Lt Gane proceeded on leave to England. 2 O.R. attached to 15th Squadron R.F.C. for aeroplane signalling. 8 N.C.O.'s joined Brigade Bombing class.	
"	3-1-17		Training carried on. 1 O.R. proceeded to ETAPLES for Lewis Gun Course. Honor Rev N Evans proceeded to England for Commission.	
"	4-1-17		Training.	
"	5-1-17		Training carried on. 2nd Lt Joyce and 16 O.R. returned from Lewis Gun School ETAPLES. 8 N.C.O.s rejoined from Brigade Bombing class. 1 O.R. joined from Lewis Gun School ETAPLES.	
"	6-1-17		Training. 2nd Lt Sutton & 2 O.R. rejoined from Divisional School.	
"	7-1-17		SUNDAY. 11 N.C.O.s rejoined from Divisional Bombing Class.	
"	8-1-17		Training.	
"	9-1-17	9.15 am	Battalion moved to AUTHIEUL. Rendezvous, Cross Roads N.E. end of village. Inspection of the Battalion on the march by Divisional Commander. AUTHIEUL 11.29 am. Fair billets. Major O'Sullivan returned off leave from England.	

Army Form C. 2118

WAR DIARY
or
INTELLIGENCE SUMMARY
(Erase heading not required.)

Instructions regarding War Diaries and Intelligence Summaries are contained in F.S. Regs., Part II. and the Staff Manual respectively. Title Pages will be prepared in manuscript.

Place	Date	Hour	Summary of Events and Information	Remarks and references to Appendices
AUTHIEUL	10-1-17		Battalion moved to SAILLY-AU-BOIS by bus. Rendezvous junction of AUTHIEUL-DOULLENS-SARTON Road 9.30 a.m. to move off 9.45 a.m. Buses arrived 11.30 p.m. Commenced journey 11.40 a.m. arrived SAILLY-AU-BOIS 12.30 p.m. Very slow proceeding but good weather. "A" and "B" Coys relieved 16th "D" West Yorkshire Regiment, 31st Division in HEBUTERNE KEEP. "C" and "D" Coys in billets at SAILLY-AU-BOIS. Trenches in the Keep in very bad condition. Casualties 4 O.R. killed. 4 O.R. wounded. Shelling.	A
SAILLY-AU-BOIS and HEBUTERNE KEEP.	11-1-17		2nd Lt. J. Bell. 1 O.R. joined. 2nd Lt. Enrighyn Scrupl. 1. O.R. to Liph. Gen. Hosp. no Cert. Lieut Meredith to 94th Infantry Brigade for training in Lewis Gunies. Lt. Col. A. Easton-de-Hoast left Battalion to take over command of 19th Infantry Brigade. Coys cleaning billets and repairing trenches. Enemy's Artillery fairly active. Our Artillery bombarded enemy's lines from 7 a.m. to about 9 a.m. Casualties: - 1 O.R. Died of Wounds.	A
SAILLY-AU-BOIS and HEBUTERNE KEEP.	12-1-17		Coys repairing billets & trenches and erecting dumps. Enemy's Artillery quiet. No 79643 C.Q.M.S. Hood to England for Commission. 1.O.R. to base for work on munitions.	A
—	13-1-17		Coys repairing billets & trenches and erecting dumps. Enemy's Artillery quiet. 2/Lt Sheeyte & 2/Lieuten John rejoin from leave. Coy Commanders viewed front line trenches. Captain Elton & Captain Gill & 9 O.R. joined Battalion	A

Army Form C. 2118

WAR DIARY
or
INTELLIGENCE SUMMARY
(Erase heading not required.)

Instructions regarding War Diaries and Intelligence Summaries are contained in F. S. Regs., Part II. and the Staff Manual respectively. Title Pages will be prepared in manuscript.

Place	Date	Hour	Summary of Events and Information	Remarks and references to Appendices
SAILLY AU BOIS and HEBUTERNE KEEP	14-1-14		Repairing Wires etc. Artillery Quiet.	
IN TRENCHES	15-1-14		Cpt Jeans returned from leave. F.G.C.M. on No 9314 L/Cpl Dartham at Bn Hd Qrs 10 A.M. Battalion moved from SAILLY-AU-BOIS to front line trenches, "C" + "D" Coys in trenches very tired, situation normal, very little rifle fire.	
—	16-1-14		Repairing Dugouts + renewing trenches. Very quiet.	
—	17-1-14		Hostile Artillery very quiet. Few shells fell in HEBUTERNE. Trenches + Dug-outs repaired.	
—	18-1-14		Repairing trenches + Dugouts. Enemy Artillery fairly active 6 to 8 o'c p.m., otherwise quiet. Major J.E.C. Thomas to Hospital.	
—	19-1-14		Trenches repaired. Enemy Artillery fairly active from 12.30 p.m. to 10 o'c a.m., directed on HEBUTERNE. Capt Smith returned off leave.	
—	20-1-14		Repairing Communication trench + front line. Enemy Artillery fairly active. Patrol under Lieut Clarke had contact with enemy party. 2 O.R. wounded, enemy dispersed. 6. O.R.s on leave.	
—	21-1-14		Enemy Artillery more active on our front line. Our light guns dispersed enemy parties seen near STAR WOOD. 3 Patrols went out to gain touch laterally, saw no enemy. Damaged front line repaired and advanced posts wired. Work with RE's in Dugouts continued. HEBUTERNE heavily shelled Gas Shell. 1 O.R. killed and 2 O.R. gassed.	

Army Form C. 2118

WAR DIARY
or
INTELLIGENCE SUMMARY
(Erase heading not required.)

Instructions regarding War Diaries and Intelligence Summaries are contained in F.S. Regs., Part II. and the Staff Manual respectively. Title Pages will be prepared in manuscript.

Place	Date	Hour	Summary of Events and Information	Remarks and references to Appendices
IN TRENCHES.	22-1-14		Work on dugouts continued. Enemy quieter today. Battalion relieved by the East Lancashire Regiment, and marched into Reserve at COURCELLES.	
COURCELLES	23-1-14		Inspection of Rifles etc. and New Billets. Church Parade the Battalion found to be 4 times less than that of other battalions in the Brigade.	
—	24-1-14		Draft of J.O.R. joined. General Training carried out. No. 14854 C.S.M. Bewley to England for a Commission.	
—	25-1-14		Brigade Tactical Scheme carried out. 2nd Lt Clarke & 2nd Lt Etherill to Hospital. 2nd Lt Whipple & 2nd Lt Owen & 4 O.R.s on leave.	
—	26-1-14		General Training. New attack formation. 'A' Coy to DELL Baths. No. 13412 CQMS Pierce to England for Commission.	
—	27-1-14		2 Companies, Working Parties, remainder General Training.	
—	28-1-14	2pm	'A' & 'B' Coys practising the Brigade Tactical Exercise. 'C' & 'D' Coys working parties at COLINCAMPS and COURCELLES. Improvement of Billets, bunking, oven building etc.	
—	29-1-14	10 AM TO 12-30	'A' & 'B' Coys again practice Brigade Exercise. Remainder of Battalion working party & improvement of billets.	

Army Form C. 2118

WAR DIARY
or
INTELLIGENCE SUMMARY

(Erase heading not required.)

Instructions regarding War Diaries and Intelligence Summaries are contained in F. S. Regs., Part II. and the Staff Manual respectively. Title Pages will be prepared in manuscript.

Place	Date	Hour	Summary of Events and Information	Remarks and references to Appendices
COURCELLES	30-1-14		Tactical Exercises last practice by A & B Coys. Working Parties C & D Coys.	
—	31-1-14		Battalion take part in attack by Brigade, viewed by General Knight fifth So. A. Army. Afternoon, Billet improvement	

H. Dakeyn Lieut Col.
Commanding 8th In North Staffordshire Regt.

WAR DIARY or INTELLIGENCE SUMMARY

8th Battalion North Staffordshire Regiment

Army Form C. 2118

Vol 20

Place	Date	Hour	Summary of Events and Information	Remarks and references to Appendices
COURCELLES AU-BOIS	1-2-४		H.R.H. Prince of Wales K.C.M.G. visited the 13th Lunched with the Officers at 1 pm, and Inspected the Batt and S'mark Frost at 2.15 pm. Div Band in attendance. R/2t Rogan proceeded on a Bombing Course.	
"	2-"-		One Company working at COLIN CAMP STATION, one Coy at R.E. Yard COURCELLES. Two Coy's practise the assault from 10 am to 12 noon. Bombing of Billets from 2 to 4 pm. 2 Officers to Heavy Artillery Group	
"	3-"-		Two Coys supplied working parties. Several enemy aeroplanes over 13th Billets. Two officers rejoined from Field Ambulance. 2/Lt Clarke and Cottrill. 13th Divisional Reserve.	19.14
"	4-"-		Special attack training C Coy. A & D Coys working parties. Draft of 4 other Ranks joined 2 Officers to H.A.G	
"	5-"-		93rd in Brigade Reserve. 3 Coys Working Parties 1 Coy in attack training. Officers View Beautine. Capt Gibson to Field Ambulance.	
"	6-"-		3 Coys working parties building Y.M.C.A Hut etc. 2 Additional Tewobans raised making in all 14.	
Trenches	7-"-		13th relieved 10 R WAR R in Butler L1. South of HEBUTERNE. Situation normal, trenches any owing to continued frost. 2nd in Command Major Thomas from S'Clore Reg't Lt Clarke left with Transport	
"	8-"-		2 Platoons supplied carrying T M bombs for coming operation. Digging impossible owing to intense frost. Our front line heavily bombarded between 7.30 pm and 9 pm. 2/Lt Clarke joined his coy in place of 2/Lt Snape. Whittle & Owen returned from leave. Situation quiet throughout the day, but heavy enemy bombardment again at night 5 killed and 13 wounded. A & B Coys relieved C & D Coys in front line. Reinforcements arrived. 2/Lt Bucklands and 94 O.R.	

1875. Wt. W5193/826 1,000,000 4/15 J.B.C. & A. A.D.S.S./Forms/C. 2118.

Army Form C. 2118

WAR DIARY
8th (S) Battalion of 13th (North Staffordshire) Regt
INTELLIGENCE SUMMARY

(Erase heading not required.)

Instructions regarding War Diaries and Intelligence Summaries are contained in F.S. Regs., Part II. and the Staff Manual respectively. Title Pages will be prepared in manuscript.

Place	Date	Hour	Summary of Events and Information	Remarks and references to Appendices
Trenches Sector L1.	10-2-17		Enemy aeroplanes active over our lines. The Devil on our right attacked at 8pm and enemy retaliates on our frontwork 2 hour bombardment, and some shelling until midnight. Our front extended on right including 1 extra post.	(A)
"	11-2-17		Situation again normal. The Bn was relieved by the 10th 2 War R and proceeded to billets A, B and HQ Coys at Bertrancourt, C and D Coys at Bus.	(B)
Bus and Bertrancourt	12-2-17		General cleaning up of equipment and billets. Lewis Gun and Bombing classes carried on.	(C)
	13-2-17		2½ Coys bombing parties, 1½ Coys at Bath, Lg and bombing classes continued. Others proceeded to AMIENS returning same evening.	(D)
Bus to Bertrancourt	14-2-17		2½ Coys working parties, 1½ Coys at Bath. Instructional classes continued. Major O'Sullivan and 2 OR departed for CALAIS. Capt Gibson reported from Fld Ambce.	(E)
" and Trenches	15-2-17		Bn inspected in key Coys by Brigadier, at 11am and 11.45am. Drew drill over. Proceeded to trenches at 3pm and relieved 10th R War R in sector L1. Right Coy got in. Capt Colls sick, left with transport.	(F)
"	16-2-17		Trenches still frozen, situation normal. 2nd Lt Gough joined Bn remaining sick transport. Enemy aeroplane brought down on our left. Work done by support Coys on Summary line and communication trenches.	(G)
" and Bertrancourt	17-2-17		Situation quiet. The Bn was relieved by 5th N Stk R and proceeded to billets in Bus and Bertrancourt. 2nd Lt Khitle and 10 OR on courses.	(H)
Bertrancourt and Bus	18-2-17		General cleaning up. Divine service in Bus Church and at Z camp.	(J)

Army Form C. 2118

WAR DIARY

8th (S) Battalion of Pr. of S.t North Staffordshire Regt

INTELLIGENCE SUMMARY

(Erase heading not required.)

Place	Date	Hour	Summary of Events and Information	Remarks and references to Appendices
Bus and BERTRANCOURT.	19-2-17		Companies paraded for Platoon & Coy drill. Rifle Bearers and Musketry attack formation. Bombing & L. Gun classes continued. The afternoon devoted to drainage of camp & transport lines. 3 platoons for working parties. Major B. Thomas elected Lt Col M.G. Instructor under Brig. orders.	
do	20-2-17		Coys paraded for drill as yesterday. Signalling class commenced and L.G. and Bombing classes continued. Bombing parties found 3 platoons to work from 8 am to 4.30 pm.	
do	21-2-17		Company training and instructional classes continued on yesterday. Working parties found 2 platoons at 8 am, 1½ Coys at 9 am, 2 platoons at 1 pm. Also 60 men to report to work to an R.E.'s officer and 2 platoons to construct Bomb Store at 9 am. Bn details for working parties with the exception of the Lewis Gun Bombing and Signalling classes. 1 O.R. court martialled at Bn H.Q.	
do	22-2-17			
"	23-2-7		Instructional classes continued. Training in new attack formation and coy and Bn drill carried on. 3 Coys to work on horse lines extra trench from 1 platoon found an working party 3 platoon of C Coy carried out Coy training, also Bombing. Signalling classes continued. New class commences under 2 Lt Beech on Rifle Grenade course. 1 O.R. from 8 Glos R attached to A Coy for duty.	
"	24-2-7		1 Platoon found on working party from 8 am. Bombing, Lewis Gun and Rifle Grenade commences under 2 Lt Beech. 1 O.R. from 8 Glos R. attached to A Coy for duty.	

1875 W1. W593/826 1,000,000 4/15 J.B.C. & A. A.D.S.S./Forms/C. 2118.

WAR DIARY
8th (S) Battalion 1st (North Staffordshire) Regt
INTELLIGENCE SUMMARY

Army Form C. 2118

Place	Date	Hour	Summary of Events and Information	Remarks and references to Appendices
Serches	25-2-17	3am	The Bn was ordered to move into the front line Sector 1.0 in support to the 8th Glos R who had advanced into vacated enemy territory. Situation normal. Heavy mist curtailed movement across the open.	MAP. REF. HEBUTERNE 1/10000
		4pm	The Bn advanced without casualties and held line extending from SERRE along SERRE B. ROAD to about junction of FRITZ AVENUE and WALTER TRENCH. During the night the line was consolidated and touch obtained with 7th & 10th on our right.	
"	26-2-17		A and C Coys advanced through the 8th Glos R and held line from junction of JERRE ALLEY and RHINE TRENCH to K24 B97 where touch	
		6am	was gained with B Coy holding line vir STAR WOOD and SLIM TRENCH to LA LOUVIERE FARM, and also on right with 31st Divn.	
		7am	Patrol sent out to BOX WOOD from B Coy have established a post there. C Coy attempted to advance on PUISIEUX but held up by MG fire at about 1000 yds range. No casualties. RHINE TRENCH consolidated.	
"	27-2-17		10 Coy moved into support on SERRE B. ROAD. Bn relieved at dawn by 10 R. WAR. and proceeded to EUSTON, moving into hellos at 4 pm. 2 officers joined Bn for duty.	
COURCELLES	28-2-17		General cleaning of equipment etc. Signalling class continued. 2 Coys sent to COLINCAMPS to unload trucks.	

Army Form C. 2118

WAR DIARY
or
INTELLIGENCE SUMMARY

8th (S) Batt^n The Prince of Wales's North Staffordshire Regiment

(Erase heading not required.)

Instructions regarding War Diaries and Intelligence Summaries are contained in F.S. Regs., Part II. and the Staff Manual respectively. Title Pages will be prepared in manuscript.

Vol 21

Place	Date	Hour	Summary of Events and Information	Remarks and references to Appendices
COURCELLES	1-3-17		Regt^l Classes carried on. Remainder of Batt^n on Docking Party laying Railway. Capt Bull to Englaston	
"	2-"-		As for 1st	
"	3-"-		do for 1st	
"	4-"-		do for 1st	
"	5-"-		do for 1st	
"	6-"-		do for 1st	
"	7-"-		do for 1st	
"	8-"-		Regt^l Classes carried on. General cleaning up ready for move on the 9th	
"			All L.S.A. except 10 Rds per man also bombs returned to Divisional Bomb Stores about 9 hrs arr. also Lewis Gun Equipment. Lieut Muir joined Batt^n	
COURCELLES & LOUVENCOURT	9-"-	9.45 AM	Bn moved to Louvencourt during the frost the marching became bad. Arrived LOUVENCOURT 11-15am Lieut ORROM joined Batt^n	
-"- and GEZAINCOURT	10-3-17	9.30 AM	Bn moved to GEZAINCOURT. Roads very bad in places otherwise good marching. arrived GEZAINCOURT 1-45 P.M.	
-"- and BONNIERS	11-3-17	9.am	Bn marched to BONNIERS. Good marching. Fine weather arrived BONNIERS 12.10 Pm Good Billets	
BONNIERS	12-3-17		Resting and General cleaning up. raining all day.	
-"- and CROISETTE	13-"-		Bn marched to CROISETTE and WIGNACOURT. Good marching and good weather arrived junction of CROISETTE & Wignacourt 12.15 P.m. D Coy billeted in Wignacourt	
WIGNACOURT	"-			

WAR DIARY
8th B" North Staffordshire Regiment
INTELLIGENCE SUMMARY

Army Form C. 2118

Place	Date	Hour	Summary of Events and Information	Remarks and references to Appendices
CROISETTE to WIGNACOURT	14.2.17	8-30a	B" marched to HESTRUS. Raining practically all the way. Arrived HESTRUS 12.10 P.m.	1
HESTRUS	15-"-		General cleaning up. Inspection of companies by C.O. in the afternoon.	
HESTRUS to EQUEDECQUES	16-"-	4-p.m.	B" moved to EQUEDECQUES and LES PRESSES. Good marching. C & D Coys billeted at LES PRESSES.	1
LES PRESSES				
-"- to THINNES	17-"-	6.55a.	B" marched to THINNES. A little rain fell en route. Arrived THINNES 1-30 P.m. B" spread out over a distance of about 3 kilometres. 2/Lt. FERGUSON posted to B" but admitted to hospital at BETHUNE	1
THINNES to MERRIS	18-"-	9-30a	B" marched to MERRIS AREA. Roads good. Halted for dinners at 1 P.m. moved off again at 2 P.m. Arrived MERRIS AREA at 4-30 P.m.	1
MERRIS	19-"-		B" resting and general cleaning up.	
MERRIS	20-"-		Coys carried out drill & inspection. The C.O. 2 Officers and 1 W.O. per Coy proceeded to 11 E.W. DEPENDAAL sector prior to going into the line. 3 officers & O.Rs joined 15 & 2/Lt Shirly & Ruttes.	1
MERRIS to RIDGEWOOD	21.3.17	7.20a	B" marched to RIDGEWOOD and relieved the 10" Queens Regt, arrived at the wood 11-15a.m. A little shelling occurred during the day no casualty.	1
RIDGEWOOD	22.3.17		The enemy shelled RIDGEWOOD about 4.30p.m. Capt Williams wounded in dugout. Two Coys to Canal bo Pop.	1
TRENCHES	22.3.17	6.30a	B" relieved 26" Royal Fusiliers in trenches. Left Sector DEPENDAAL Sector. No hostile firing during relief. D Coy front line. B Coy New Reserve Line C Coy in Redoubt & S.P.7 O Coy in Lilly Hollow.	1
TRENCHES	23.3.17		Very little hostile firing. B Coy carried out wiring of front line P & O trench.	1

Army Form C. 2118

WAR DIARY
8 (S) Batt. North Staffordshire Regiment
INTELLIGENCE SUMMARY
(Erase heading not required.)

Instructions regarding War Diaries and Intelligence Summaries are contained in F.S. Regs., Part II. and the Staff Manual respectively. Title Pages will be prepared in manuscript.

Place	Date	Hour	Summary of Events and Information	Remarks and references to Appendices
Trenches	24-3-17		Very little trouble through enemy fire. B Coy relieved A Coy in front line. relief complete by 9 p.m.	
"	25 " "		Very quiet on the whole except that 6 Trench Mortars very active from 9:30 P.m. to 10 P.m. a little damage done to front line trench. Casualties 9 wounded.	
"	26 " "		Little artillery activity but quiet on the whole. Lt Whittle + a few men entered the German front line but saw no signs of any of the enemy. 1 O.R. wounded.	
Trenches Ridgewood	27 " "		B" relieved in Trenches by 10" R.W.R. Relief complete by 12.9.P.R. Very quiet enemy. relief. B" + A Co A + B Coy proceeded to MURRUM BIDGE-EE Camp. LA CLYTTE. C + D under Major Thomas remain in RIDGEWOOD, as supports and to find working parties.	
LA CLYTTE	28 " "		Right half Battalion Training. Left half working parties.	
"	29 " "		Training carried on. C.O. + O.Coys working parties. 10 officers from Capt R.CHALLONER.M.C. attached from J.Lewis Regt and posted to O.Coys. 2 Lt Gough + 2.O.Rs rejoined from Divisional School. Brigadier gave a lecture in MURRUM BIDGE-EE camp on: History of PRUSSIA.	
"	30 " " and		B" relieved by 6 Nishins and Welsh Regt respecting. Right Half B" + forms and Left Half of the latter. Right Half Batt. arrived at PH IN C BOOM at 5.45 P.m. Left Half at 6 + 5 P.m.	
PH IN C BOOM	31 " "		General cleaning up for C + O Coys. A + B Coys carried out Training Classes. 2 + 61 O.Rs rejoined from various Schools. Capt G. Wood to Hospital.	

J. L. Sahgin
Lieut.-Col.
Commanding 8th (S) Batt. North Stafford Regt.

To 57 Infy Bde

Herewith War Diary
for April 1917

W Shakespeare Major
                    Lieut.-Col.
Commanding 8th (S) Batt. North Stafford Regt.

Army Form C. 2118

WAR DIARY
8th (S) Battalion of North Staffordshire Regiment
INTELLIGENCE SUMMARY

(Erase heading not required.)

Vol 22

Place	Date	Hour	Summary of Events and Information	Remarks and references to Appendices
RHINE BOOM	1-4-17		Sunday. Two Officers joined Bn. 2nd Lts P.G. GOUGH + J.S. MAGUIRE.	
RHINE BOOM & HAZEBROUCH	2-4-17	9.40am	Bn moved to HAZEBROUCH. Good marching arrived HAZEBROUCH 12.20pm	
" "	3rd	8.20am	Bn marched to ST MARTIN AU LAERT. Very heavy snow storm for first two miles. Heavy marching throughout, arrived ST MARTIN 2.10pm.	
ST MARTIN AU LAERT & SETQUES	4"	2pm	Bn moved to SETQUES. Good marching arrived SETQUES 4.35pm	
SETQUES	5"	8.30am	Bn marched to MORINGHEM. arrived MORINGHEM 10.10am. The New ZEALAND Rifle Brigade had also received orders to billet in these villages. Bn waited on the road until 2.30p.m. when definite orders were received to occupy villages. Bn Hd Qrs & D Coy billetted in MORINGHEM. A Coy Gd DIFQUES and B & C Coys in PT DIFQUES.	
MORINGHEM Gd & PT DIFQUES				
MORINGHEM Gd & PT DIFQUES	6"		General cleaning up & training.	
" - "	7"		Training carried on. Capt H.R. SELFE joined Bn with 3 other ranks	
" - "	8"		Sunday. A little training after Divine Service. 2nd Lt R. Shackleton joined Bn from G.H.Q. Cadet School	
" - "	9"		Training continued	
" - "	10"		ditto	
" - "	11"		Training. It was very wet and snow fell great part of the day	
" - "	12"		Training	
" - "	13		ditto. 2nd Lt Hancock travelled on leave to England	

Army Form C. 2118

WAR DIARY
8 Bn N.th or Staffs Regt
INTELLIGENCE SUMMARY
(Erase heading not required.)

Instructions regarding War Diaries and Intelligence Summaries are contained in F.S. Regs., Part II. and the Staff Manual respectively. Title Pages will be prepared in manuscript.

Place	Date	Hour	Summary of Events and Information	Remarks and references to Appendices
MORINGHEM 6th Pt D1 PQUE	14-4-17		Training carried on	
-"-	15"		" - " - "	
-"-	16"		" - " - "	
ST MARTIN AU LAERT	17"	9 am	Bn moved to ST. MARTIN AU LAERT. Good march arrived destination 11-20am	
-"- and HAZEBROUCH	18"	7-45am	Bn moved again to HAZEBROUCH. A little rain. Arrived HAZEBROUCH 3-15 pm	
-"- and DE ZON Camp	19"	7-30am	Bn marched to DE ZON Camp. Situated M.12 A & 9. Map. BEL + FRANCE. Sheet 28. 1:40000 arrived in Camp at 4. pm. Very good accommodation for all ranks.	
-"-	20"		Training carried on. and working parties under Div. Sig. Officer for cable burying	— 1 — 1
-"-	21st		ditto	— 1 — 1
-"-	22nd		" - " - "	— — 2 Other Ranks
-"-	23"		Proceeded on courses of instruction. So far 20: 1 Officer & 5 other Ranks proceeded on Courses of instruction.	
-"- and BETHEN	24"	2 pm	Training & working parties carried on. C + D Coys moved to BETHEN and attached to SF Infy Bde for training in mopping up cluster.	attached 9 P W F40, 6 with D — 6 with
-"-	25		Training Carried on.	

Army Form C. 2118

WAR DIARY
or
INTELLIGENCE SUMMARY

(Erase heading not required.)

Instructions regarding War Diaries and Intelligence Summaries are contained in F. S. Regs., Part II and the Staff Manual respectively. Title Pages will be prepared in manuscript.

Place	Date	Hour	Summary of Events and Information	Remarks and references to Appendices
DE ZOH CAMP	26/7		Training carried on.	
" "	27		" " "	
" "	28		Lt Col Baloyne proceeded on leave	
" "	29		" " "	
" and SCOTTISH CAMP G.23 A 8.6	30		B˚ moved to Scottish camp situated G.23 A 8.6. M.P. Belgium trans sheet 28. 1/40000. Approx'd distination 6.50 P.m.	

Commanding 8th

1875 Wt. W 593/826 1,000,000 4/15 J.B.C.& A. A.D.S.S./Forms/C. 2118.

WAR DIARY or INTELLIGENCE SUMMARY

8 (S) Batt" North Staffordshire Regiment

Vol 23

Army Form C. 2118

Place	Date	Hour	Summary of Events and Information	Remarks and references to Appendices
SCOTTISH LINES G25 A 8.6. BELGIUM + FRANCE 1/40,000	1.5.17		Training carried on.	
SCOTTISH LINES + Trenches	2.5.17	7.30 PM	Bn. Marched from SCOTTISH LINES to trenches + relieved 8th BATTN. YORK & LANCASTER REGT- in the Left Subsector (HILL 60 Sector). MAP ZILLEBEKE 28NW 1/10,000 Right boundary J.29.b.9.2. J.29.b.9.2. A NE 3 Part 4A Left boundary J.24.d.6.5.1.0. C Coy RIGHT FRONT " J.24.d.6.5.1.0. D " LEFT " B " in Support A + Left with 9th G Hodkins in Reserve. Joined up on RIGHT with 10th Worcesters on Left with 9th G Hodkins Enemy was very quiet during and after relief which was completed by 2.47 AM 3/5/17. 1 O.R. wounded. Gas alarm sounded about 10.15 P.M (from direction of ST JEANE) which delayed the relief considerably. Enemy quiet during relief. He fired 20 H.E in the vicinity of Battn HQs destroying one M.G Emplacement. 4 O.R's killed, 1 wounded of S Bdge M.G Coy.	
TRENCHES	3.5.17		Artillery on both sides quiet during the day. 1 O.R wounded.	
TRENCHES	4.5.17		Nothing to report very little shelling. 1 O.R wounded	
TRENCHES	5.5.17		Enemy Artillery active Considerable increase during the 10.30-12.24 hours Enemy nothing unusual 30 officers found at transport (2 Lts 1 food, Robey and Panthorn) otherwise nothing unusual to report. MAJOR Shakespeare to Hospital. MAJOR Zulf Gerald 10 R. warwicks Regt took temporary command of	
TRENCHES	7.5.17		the Batn. all was quiet Artillery opened fire on enemys trenches from 8.45 - 8.50.P.M and 11.15 - 11.30. P.M.	
TRENCHES	8.5.17		Quiet occasional burst of enemy artillery 3 O.R. wounded.	

WAR DIARY or INTELLIGENCE SUMMARY

Army Form C. 2118

8th (S) Batt. North Staffordshire Regt

Place	Date	Hour	Summary of Events and Information	Remarks and references to Appendices
TRENCHES	9/5/17		Comparatively quiet. Enemy Snipers very active. Enemy Artillery heavily bombarded vicinity of Batt. H.Qrs. expected from 9.30 to 10.20 P.M. - a light bombardment at 3.30 AM nothing followed. 10 Wounded at B.Saus. 3.O.R. killed. 9 wounded.	
TRENCHES	10/5/17		Very quiet. Batn. relieved by 13th Batn D.L.I. relief commenced at 11.30 P.M.	
SCOTTISH LINES + WESTON CAMP	G.23.B.1.9 11/5/17		Relief completed without interruption from Enemy at 3 AM Battn. afterwards moved to SCOTTISH LINES arrived 6.30 AM Battn. moved to WESTON CAMP SHARPENBURG AREA. M.17.D.3.8. arrived WESTON CAMP. 5.10 PM.	
WESTON CAMP	12/5/17		Very hot - weather. General clean up. Divine Service. Major J. Fitzgerald rejoins 10th R. Warwicks Regt. Capt. Gibson assumes temporary command of the Battn.	
WESTON CAMP	13/5/17		Training carried on. Lt Col H. O. Daley & Lt Col H.O. Dakeyne rejoined from leave.	
WESTON CAMP	14/5/17		Training carried on. 2nd Lt. D.O. Jones admitted to Hospital.	
WESTON CAMP	15/5/17		Training carried on A.T.B. Coy proceeded to be attached to 58 Inf Bdg & for training. 2/Lt P.G. Gough & 2/Lt Walton Capell on route for REGVE Area 2/Lt P.G. Gough admitted to Hospital	
WESTON CAMP	16/5/17		Training carried on. Draft 25 O.R. joined Battn	
"	17/5/17		Training carried on. Draft 25 O.R. joined Battn	
	18/5/17			
	19/5/17			
	20/5/17			

Army Form C. 2118

WAR DIARY
8th (S) Batt? or North Staffordshire Regt
INTELLIGENCE SUMMARY
(Erase heading not required.)

Instructions regarding War Diaries and Intelligence Summaries are contained in F.S. Regs., Part II. and the Staff Manual respectively. Title Pages will be prepared in manuscript.

Place	Date	Hour	Summary of Events and Information	Remarks and references to Appendices
WESTON CAMP	20/5/17	9 pm	Left half Batt? moved to MURRUM BRIDGE CAMP at 7 & 8.5 arrived destination 7.40 pm. Map Ref. Bel: Sheet 28 Sd 3 1/40,000.	arrived
MURRUMBR DEE CAMP	21/5/17		Training carried on.	
"	22/5/17		Every available man employed on working parties. both by day & by night.	
"	23/5/17		" " "	
"	24/5/17		Training carried on with left half Batt? A&B Co?s arrive from training attachment to 58th BdeS arrive MURRUM BRIDGE CAMP at 8pm attached 8th Batt. Gloucester Regt. A+B Co?s move to RIDGE WOOD Map Ref. Bel: Sheet 28 S.3. 1/40,000. Ry. N 64+13 Map Ref. Bel: Sheet 28. C.6. 1/40,000. RIGHT half Batt. Half MURRUM BRIDGE Co?s P in reserve LEFT half Batt. RIDGEWOOD Rest. Half MURRUM BRIDGE Co?s P in reserve	
RIDGE WOOD MURRUM BRIDGE CAMP. TRENCHES	25/5/17		The Batt. relieved the 10th B Warwicks R in Left sub-sector (Kruisenhoek) A + B in FRONT LINE from 6.10. C in SLEEPY HOLLOW D in Redoubts Right Half Bn moved from RIDGEWOOD LEFT " " " MURRUM BRIDGE CAMP at 8.15 pm Relief completed 12.15 am 26/5. Very quiet during relief.	
TRENCHES	26/5/17		Relief completed 12.15 am. Our Artillery were cutting Repairs in all Trenches carried out.	
TRENCHES	27/5/17		Trenches continued to be repaired. wire cutting by our Artillery continued. Enemy Artillery quiet in day but very active during night. 1 O.R. Killed. 3 O.R. wounded.	

Army Form C. 2118

WAR DIARY
8th (S) Batt or North Staffordshire Regt
INTELLIGENCE SUMMARY

(Erase heading not required.)

Instructions regarding War Diaries and Intelligence Summaries are contained in F.S. Regs., Part II. and the Staff Manual respectively. Title Pages will be prepared in manuscript.

Place	Date	Hour	Summary of Events and Information	Remarks and references to Appendices
TRENCHES	28/5/17		Our Artillery continued wire cutting. Enemy Artillery very active during night. 4 O.R. wounded.	
"	29/5/17		Our Artillery continued wire cutting. Trenches rifle pierced. Enemy Artillery active from 10PM. 3 O.R. wounded. The Battn was relieved by 7th S. Lancs Regt commencing at 9.45PM completed at 1.AM 30th.	
TRENCHES / KEMPTON CAMP	30/5/17		On relieving completed the Battn moved to KEMPTON CAMP arrived 3 AM end of day. Several Clean up 28 SW S7 30&10 M.14 to 9.7.	
KEMPTON CAMP	31/5/17		Battn. Training carried on. 2nd Lt H.S. Gough rejoined from leave.	

H. S. Dalrymple Lt. Col.
Commanding 8th (S) Battn N. Staford Regt.

WAR DIARY

Army Form C. 2118

8th (S) Batt. INTELLIGENCE SUMMARY North Staffordshire Regt.

Vol 24

Place	Date	Hour	Summary of Events and Information	Remarks and references to Appendices
KEMPTON PARK CAMP.	1/6/17		Battalion Training carried on. 2nd Lts P.G. Gough to Royal Flying Corps. 2nd Lts C. Shirley and 2 O.Rs. reported from courses.	
BELGIUM + FRANCE SHEET 28 Edition 3. M 14.c.9.7. 1/40,000	2/6/17		Inspection of 57th INFANTRY BDE by Major Gen. D.B. SHUTE C.B., C.M.G. commdg. 19th Divn. Battalion Training continued. Two officers joined viz. Major W.D. SWORD (1st Battn) as 2nd in Command. + 2/Lt M.G. RANDALL 1/6 A Coy.	
	3/6/17		Battn Training Continued. 2nd Lt Whittle, 2nd Lt G.L. Robey to courses. Lt J.C.W. Boulton reported from leave.	
	4/6/17		Bde Training carried out. Attack Scheme. Major W.D. Sword to Divl Reinforcement Camp as O.C.	
	5/6/17		Bde attack scheme carried out. Lecture on barrage to Officers of Bde by Brigadier Gen. Monkhouse C.R.A. Major G.P. Smith returned from leave.	
"and Assembly Area M12.b.1.9 REFERENCE BELGIUM + FRANCE Edition 3a	6/6/17		The Battn moved from Kempton Brown Assembly Area to Assembly Area arrived 12.30 P.M. Battn moved from Assembly Area to Assembly trenches at 10.10 P.M. Assembly trenches 28. S.W. to.000. Relief complete 07a 1.8 15 O.I.C. 6.K. Ref WYTSCHAETE.	
Reference WYTSCHAETE 28.5.W. 10,000	7/6/17		at 2.15 A.M. I.O.R. missing. The 19th Divn is to attack the German position from old German front line between 076.9.7. and 0.18.6.3.6 to BLACK LINE between 0.15.c.50.95. and 0.20.a.35.90. The 49th Bde. 16th Divn were on the right of the 19th Divn and the 124 Bde. 41st Divn were on the left. The 11 Sth R Warwicks on the 10th Corps. The 19th D Warwicks and the left attacking Divn of the 9th Corps. Objectives of 19th Divn 58th Infantry Bage on its right, 56th Infantry Bage on the left.	

WAR DIARY
or
INTELLIGENCE SUMMARY

Army Form C. 2118

8"(S) Batt North Staffordshire Regt

Place	Date	Hour	Summary of Events and Information	Remarks and references to Appendices
Reference WYSCHAETE 28 S.W.	7/6/17		The 56th, 58th Bdges objectives were the RED BLUE & GREEN Lines. The 57th Bdge were to attack and capture the BLACK LINE. ZERO HOUR for 56th + 58th Bdges. 3.10 A.M. Objective. The Battn advanced from the assembly trenches in Artillery formation at 3.40 P.M. (ZERO plus 2 hrs 30 mins). Front Coys A and B. Rear Coys C and D and Battn HQrs. The old British I line was crossed at 3.50 (ZERO plus 2 hrs 40 mins) and advance continued on to BLUE LINE which was reached at 6.50 a.m (ZERO plus 3 hrs 40 mins) MAP REFERENCE E. BLUE LINE in O. 8. c and d. Battn remained here for 20 minutes when direction etc. etc were checked. At 7.10 a.m. (Zero plus 4 hours) the advance to the GREEN LINE was commenced. Two hundred yards from the Battn the Enemy out-posts formation. The GREEN LINE was reached at 7.50 (ZERO plus 4 hrs 40 mins) Reference. O.14.b.9.5.6.0 to O.14.b.5.0.3.0. The two leading Coys (A and B) crossed GREEN LINE and halted 100 yds in front of it, the two rear Coys halting behind it. At 8.10 AM the BLACK LINE was assaulted between O.15.C.55.90 and O.14.d.75.95. This line was completed captured by 8.30 AM. Very few casualties + little resistance was offered by the enemy. The tendency of the enemy was to rush forward + surrender on before very few actually stayed in the trenches. Two platoons of C.D. Coys at once passed through the French line on the MAUVE LINE	

1875 Wt. W593/826 1,000,000 4/15 J.B.C. & A. A.D.S.S./Forms/C.2118.

WAR DIARY or INTELLIGENCE SUMMARY

Army Form C. 2118

8th (S) Batt. North Staffordshire Regt.

Place	Date	Hour	Summary of Events and Information	Remarks and references to Appendices

Advance WYSCHAETE — 7/6/17

Morning N.E. side of OOSTTAVERNE WOOD. Up to this time 80–100 prisoners had passed through our hands including 4 Officers. From 8·20 A.M. 15·2·30 P.M. Consolidation was carried on & M.G. Coys dug themselves in on a line 100 YDS in front of its old BLACK LINE. Wiring etc. advanced. Lewis Gun posts were made & manned. Parties were pushed forward to search OOSTAVERNE WOOD and in one or two cases fired batches of snipers were brought out. Patrols were sent out before the MAUVE LINE one of which was through on barrage into OOSTAVERNE VILLAGE and brought back valuable information. At 2·40 P.M further Operation orders were received ordering capture and consolidation of ODONTO TRENCH in O.16.c + O.22.a by the 57th B·58. In order of advance 1st Royal Warwickshire Regt Left front line

8th Glosts Regt. " Right "

8th N. Staffords " in Support

10th Worcesters " in Reserve.

ZERO HOUR 3·10 PM
At 3·5 AM the 9th S. Lancs Regt. came to relieve the Batts in the BLACK LINE Baths.
At 3·10 PM the advanced on ODONTO TRENCH. Owing to the 8th Glosts not having received orders their Coy. on the Right, although found us were the front line on the Right + although in support the Blue Line in O.22.a. Very few casualties captured and very

WAR DIARY or INTELLIGENCE SUMMARY

8th (S) Batt. The Shefford Regt

Place	Date	Hour	Summary of Events and Information	Remarks and references to Appendices
Reference Wyschaete	7/6/17		Little resistance. Two - 60 Prisoners captured including two Officers also 3 Field Guns at O.21.6.10.85. On ODONTO TRENCH being captured. Our Coys were withdrawn to a position on the E of OOSTTAVERNE VILLAGE and the work of consolidation was vigorously carried on. At 5 P.M. J. was reported our barrage was falling short actually into our front-line trenches particularly on the right in O.27.a. This compelled the Ghurkas to withdraw to a line in OOSTTAVERNE VILLAGE. The ODONTO LINE was again recovered by downing Bn Hqs. Situated at O.21.b.20.95. After ODONTO TRENCH had been recaptured considerable numbers of enemy were seen to retire across the open country. The was immediately passed to the Artillery who opened a Shrapnel barrage on them. Slight wounded remained with Unit Officers Capt G. Armstrong R.A.M.C. 2Lt G.Ough + 2Lt J. Bell. O.R.s killed 4. Wounded 69. Missing 4. During the night enemy was fairly quiet although OOSTTAVERNE ROAD in O.15.c. + d. was heavily shelled (D).	
	8/6/17.		Works of consolidation carried on. Enemy snipers very active in front of ODONTO TRENCH and considerably hampered our men from working. A Lewis gun party under 2Lt J. Bell left our line to clear trench snipers out of Bung. enfo. shell holes etc and other places	

Place	Date	Hour	Summary of Events and Information	Remarks and references to Appendices
WYTSCHAETE	8/6/17		Where they were established. Fifteen of the enemy were actually killed & any who bounded band 11 prisoners brought in. This party suffered no casualties. This raid was carried out in broad daylight & showed great skill and determination on the part of Sergt J. Bell. During the day our Trenches were not subjected to heavy fire but OOSTTAVERNE ROAD & Baths #90 at 0.6 & 95 were heavily shelled. OOSTTAVERNE WOOD also was uncomfortable. shelled throughout the day. About 8.15 P.M. the Enemy started to barrage on our whole system of Trenches both Observed & Off. + a counter attack was anticipated. On Artillery replied vigorously. At 9.30 P.M. the enemy was seen to leave his Trenches to attack us. Mg Gun fire & S. Bell had been used by our Artillery and M.Gun fire. But owing to the previous bombardment 20 of the enemy into the rear party had drawn 20 of the enemy into the ANZAC LINES where they were captures. Again we suffered no casualties. Casualties for the day. Officers wounded Capt B. J. Bell 2nd Lt H.C Maude & 2nd Lt R Shackleton wounded & missing. O.R. killed 13, wounded 35. missing 2. Baths was relieved by the 7th S. Lanes. Regt. Commencing at 10.30 P.M. Relief completed by 1.40 am Baths moved back to BLACK LINE Baths was near EVANS POST M.	

WAR DIARY or INTELLIGENCE SUMMARY

8 (S) Batt. N. Stafford Regt.

Army Form C. 2118

Place	Date	Hour	Summary of Events and Information	Remarks and references to Appendices
WYTSCHAETE	9/6/17		Works & Consolidation on the BLACK LINE. Enemy artillery quiet. OOSTTAVERNE WOOD shelled throughout the day. Wounded Officers. Capt. J. A. S. Gibson. O.R.W. 5.	
	10/6/17		Works continued on BLACK LINE. Baths moved from BLACK LINE 15 WESTON CAMP M.19.d.7.7. Commencing at 6.30 P.M. Relief completed in WESTON CAMP at 9.15.	
FRANCE 2R S.W. 5F Edition	11/6/17		General Clean up. Roll Called.	
	12/6/17		Inspection SK Bdye by Maj Gen Shute CB Croix de Gre. 19/5/17 when afterwards addressed Congratulating BGs on its gallant conduct in action against MESSINES – WYTSCHAETE RIDGE 7/6/17.	
WESTON CAMP M.19.d.77	13/6/17		Training carried on. Inspection of arms, Kits etc.	
	14/6/17		" " " "	
15/4/17	15/6/17		Batts marched to RIDGE WOOD commencing 11 o'clock and remained there for the day at 9.30 P.M. the Batts marched to the trenches and relieved the 7" Lancers in the OOSTTAVERNE SECTOR. Advanced line from O.16.d.I.4. 15.02.6.25.55. Relief completed 2.55 P.M. 1.OR wounded. Enemy artillery quiet during the day. Active at night in OOSTTAVERNE ROAD & WOOD.	
	16/6/17		Officers wounded Capt G.P. Smith OR wounded 1. Works carried out informed of wiring advanced line posts & Communication dragging Communications trench from Hqs. to FRONT LINE. Active at night. Works continued on trenches.	
	17/6/17			

Army Form C. 2118

WAR DIARY
or
INTELLIGENCE SUMMARY

(Erase heading not required.)

Instructions regarding War Diaries and Intelligence Summaries are contained in F. S. Regs., Part II. and the Staff Manual respectively. Title Pages will be prepared in manuscript.

Place	Date	Hour	Summary of Events and Information	Remarks and references to Appendices
OOSTTAVERNE SECTOR O16c3rd O 2a6.	18/6/17		Enemy Quiet during day: at 8 pm barraged on front line & attacks developed: Counterattack air activity. OOSTTAVERNE ROAD and WOOD intermittently shelled.	
	19/6/17		Quiet. Battn relieved by 9th Innishkilling Fusiliers: relief completed by 12.40 p.m. Battn marched to BIRR BARRACKS LOCRE arrived 3.40 a.m.	
R5a O.S.	20/6/17		Battn marched to Camp on R5+a O.S. at 7.40pm arrived in camp 8.50pm	
"	21/6/17		General clean up inspection of all kit arms etc.	
	22/6/17		Training carried on.	
	23/6/17		Inspection of 549 R of by L.O.C. 16th Inf. Bde. J.C.Bridge. The Corps Commander visited the Commanding Officer + congratulated Battn on work done in the recent operations	
	24/6/17		Training	
	25/6/17		Training	
	26/6/17		Battn Sports	
	27/6/17		Training + Bye Sports	
	28/6/17		Training	
	30/6/17		Training	

H.S. Dakeyne
1.VII.17

WAR DIARY
or
INTELLIGENCE SUMMARY

Army Form C. 2118

6 (S) Batt North Staffordshire Regt

Vol 25

Place	Date	Hour	Summary of Events and Information	Remarks and references to Appendices
STAFFORD CAMP R24 a 0.6 N 17a z 6	1/7/17		The Battn moved to forward area at N 17a 2 6 TRANSPORT to N 16 c 3 9 WYTSCHAETE to 0.0. Edinm Battn	
			The Battn relieved the 2/3rd 8" Lincoln Regt 65th B91 in Reserve Battn H.Qs in a 88 C and B Coys RIDGE DEFENCES	
WYTSCHAETE Section	2/7/17		O in a 88 C and B Coys RIDGE DEFENCES Relief complete 4.40 PM A & D Reserve	
1.0.0.0 Edition 3.H	3/7/17		Quiet day Battn moved forward to trenches A Coy Denys wood B Coy RAVINE WOOD D Coy PHEASANT WOOD C Coy RAVINE WOOD Batty H.Qs Regt H.Q.C 27 relieved two Coys 24th London Regt and two Coys 2/London Batty Regt 4th Division Relief complete 12.50 AM 15 Bayth Jerrald B Coy placed at disposal of O C R Warwick Regt	
	4/7/17		Quiet day B Coy placed Improvement of trenches carried on work for tactical purposes continued	
	5/7/17 6/7/17		Quiet day work on Improvement of trenches A Coy placed at disposal of O C R Warwick Regt for tactical purposes Improvement of trenches carried on the left sector R warwick Regt in the left sector	
	7/7/17		Battn relieved the 10th R Warwick Regt HQs in 15 Wood C A D Coys in front line B Coy in support Relief complete 2.50 AM	
	8/7/17		An enemy over any Sector and indiscriminate shelling throughout the day by Capt. BELL to Hospital Glad Regt on	
	9/7/17		Advance made by D Coy in conjunction with Glad Regt on night with artillery support. All objectives gained Casualties Capt SELFE Killed 3 ORs Killed 3 Wounded Improvement of	
	10/7/17		Shelling on our sector throughout the day Improvement of trenches D Coy H.Qs & H.Q. Gabion ground the Battn took command of	
	11/7/17		The Battn was relieved by the 6 West Regt (58 Bde) and moved to	

1875 Wt. W593/826 1,000,000 4/15 J.B.C. & A. A.D.S.S./Forms/C.2118.

WAR DIARY / INTELLIGENCE SUMMARY

Army Form C. 2118

8th (S) Batt'n North Stafford Regt

Place	Date	Hour	Summary of Events and Information	Remarks and references to Appendices
WYTSCHAETE SN	1/11/17		Camp at SIEGE FM. Inspection by O.C. Corps of all arms, equipment etc.	
to AOO Edition	2/11/17		Battalion clean up. Commanding officer returned from leave.	
SIEGE FM CAMP B Bn SIEGE FM	3/11/17		Batt'n clean up. Commanding officer inspected the lines.	
	14/11/17		Parades under Coy officers. Ammo Dump new attacks Bath Parades 15/11	
	15/11/17		Parades under Coy officers and 2 Lts w 3 Whitehead joined. Brigade congratulated officers & men. 2nd Batt'n attacked 6th Staffords	
	16/11/17		2/Lt P Hammond and 2/Lts W G O & 57 2nd Commanding R.A.M.C. Parades. Inspection present works Capt Armstrong Batt'n 2nd army Rest camp went on leave. Major Shakespeare joined. Capt S.M.D. 8 Officers 400 O.R. Working parties to DAMMSTRASSE PARMA VIERSTRAAT Burying Cable	D D D D
	17/11/17		Working parties vicinity of Capt J.A.S. GIBSON on leave. Parties as on the 17/11/17. Capt Brown on leave. Capt Evans joined Batt'n	D
	18/11/17 19/11/17 20/11/17		" "	
	24/11/17		1st Batt'n relieved to STANCE Regt (56 BAT'Y) A Coy in BLACK LINE Bn H'Q'rs in ONRAET WOOD B PHEASANT WOOD C FRONT OF ONRAET WOOD D MAIN LINE	
	25/11/17		B Coy came under the orders of 6th Batt'n. Relief completed 11.30 pm	D
			Battn Right Front Line carrying working parties carrying wire bombs etc.	D

(9 35 21) W 3707—598 500M 7/16 H W V [E. 195.] Forms/IV. 3121/3			Army Form W. 3121.		
Brigade.		Division.	Corps.	Date of Recommendation.	
Schedule No. (to be left blank)	Unit	Regtl. No.	Rank and Name	Action for which commended	Recommended by	Honour or Reward	(To be left blank)

Working parties continued. Quiet day.

2n[d]/L[t] J Blake wounded (slight)
remained with Unit. 6 O.R. Killed 33 wounded working Party
@ B[att]y HQ PP & Army Road C[am]p
@ 16.00 moved forward into ODONTO TRENCH owing
B[att]n being raided & suffering heavy casualties
Reorganising officer returned from near Elverd[inghe] to perform off[icer]
leave. M.O. evacuated sick.
The B[att]n relieved to 6th Gloster Regt. in its left
C+A Coys in front line R.D. in support. Relief Completed 3.30 PM
T.M.K.O. came to B[atta]lion relieved
O.C. Battn was informed by Wyves Regt. B to B
by Machine Gun troops. The Bat[tal]ion moved to YPRES BARRACKS Armoury
of dry Rifle Equipment was Inspection 6 OPs given returned of clean
The B[att]n moved to forward Camps by BEAVER CORNER in RESERVE
Army operation IV YPRES in Conjunction with 5th Army's attack.

J H Salmond Col
Comm[andin]g

8TH (S) BN PRINCE OF WALES'S (N. STAFFORD REGT) WAR DIARY AUGUST 1917

Army Form C.2118

Instructions regarding War Diaries and Intelligence Summaries are contained in F.S. Regs., Part II. and the Staff Manual respectively. Title Pages will be prepared in manuscript.

INTELLIGENCE SUMMARY
(Erase heading not required.)

Place	Date	Hour	Summary of Events and Information	Remarks and references to Appendices
Ref. Map. TRANCE 28.N.S.W.28 & BELG.SW.28	Aug 1 1917		Camp. Bde. in Reserve to 56th Bde. [consolidating positions won near GREEN Wood]. Weather very bad.	
BEAVER CORNER 28.N.15.c.9.9	2.8.17		Do:	
TRENCHES 28.O.10 & 11	2.8.17	6.30 P.M.	Batt'n by VIERSTRAAT-WYTSCHAETE & WYTSCHAETE-HOLLEBEKE roads to relieve 7 L.N. LANCS & part of 7 S. LANCS in Bde. Left Subsector Front line & Support. D Coy front line posts near FORRET Farm (Left Front) B " " " " GYM Fm & GREEN WOOD (Right Front) C " " Support (Left Support) A " " RAVINE WOOD & ROSE WOOD (Right Support) 10/WORC Regt on our Right R/SURREY " (41/Div' 122 Bde.) on our Left.	Bde. Op. Orders No. 154 Casualties Nil
Do:	4.8.17	12.30 A.M.	Relief Complete. Both Artilleries Active	
		2-4.30 A.M. 6-9 P.M.	Hostile shelling of old Front line O.11.c & Woods intense	Casualties O.R. W&M Kd. 1.
Do:	5.8.17	4 A.M. 5.20 A.M.	Patrols in early morning penetrated several 100 yards without encountering enemy. Work on wire & digging in posts. Enemy opened heavy artillery fire all calibres on old Br. front line, OLIVE TRENCH & SWITCH, & RAVINE WOOD. Accurate & intense. Determined attack on Bde. front on our left. S.O.S. put up opposite HOLLEBEKE, repeated from left front Coy site, rockets failing to go off. Thick mist prevented visibility beyond a few yards. Strength of enemy in vicinity of FORRET Fm estimated at 100. Garrison of our left two posts observed a number of men returning from FORRET Fm & being followed up by its enemy. These men were met by 2/Lt GOUGH (D.Coy B'N STAFF) on his way to left front post & informed him that their officers had been wounded. With the help of #C.S.M. ATKIS (D. Coy B'N STAFF) & 9/C.S.M of K SURREY Regt (122 Bde. Garrison of FORRET Fm) they were rallied & moved forward to deliver a counter attack on the Farm. A.M.G. opened fire from its Fm & inflicted some casualties. Garrison of left post meanwhile drove back the pursuing Germans. 2/Lt GOUGH split his party (abt 40 men) into three, sending one party to each flank	

WAR DIARY or INTELLIGENCE SUMMARY

Army Form C. 2118

Place	Date	Hour	Summary of Events and Information	Remarks and references to Appendices
Trenches	5.8.17 (cont)		flank of the F.M. & taking the centre himself. On approaching the F.M. about 50 Germans put up their hands and shouted 'Kamerad', but almost immediately laid down again & reopened fire. The three parties rushed the F.M, from which the Germans retired throwing hand grenades & firing & taking the M.G. with them. The F.M. was reoccupied & some enemy & two wounded E. SURREY officers found in the dugouts – A Lewis gun was got into action with good effect. The enemy again attacked but were driven back by L.G. & Rifle fire. Three patrols were sent out and one more prisoner brought in. Capt. COLLS (O.C. Day & N. STAFF.) meanwhile came up & took five prisoners of 89th & 98th Res. Regt & sent back five more from those captured by the E. SURREYS in the F.M. 2/Lt GOUGH took one more, a STURMTRUPPE, and a German stretcher bearer also ran into our lines – Reinforcements for the F.M. arrived from 15th Bn. HANTS Regt (41st Divn) Support Corps meantime extended their lines to protect the flanks and reinforced our front line.	
		8.30 A.M	The fog suddenly lifted and revealed abt 100 Germans equipped fully & with bayonets fixed opposite our right front Coy. They were successfully dealt with by Lewis gun & rifle fire & further demoralized by artillery fire, which opened fire an hour later by request, & obtained a direct hit on a dugout from which a number of Germans were seen to scatter.	
		6–8 A.M 6.00 A.M	Enemy's artillery fire abated considerably & reduced to normal.	
		9.30 A.M 1 P.M	Our artillery carried out several sweeping shoots on areas in front of our fronts.	
		5 P.M 9.30 P.M	A second attack on HOLLEBEKE carried out, which did not affect our front, except as regards shelling which was more intense about this time.	
		11.30 P.M	Relieved by 10th R. WAR. Regt & moved to support Trenches E of DAMSTRASSE. Bn HQ in OOSTAVERNE WOOD	Bde O. O. Nº 155 Casualties killed, 1/4 R.W. Smith/O.R. 5/ w.d. G.R. 9.

1875 Wt. W593/826 1,000,000 4/15 J.B.C. & A. A.D.S.S./Forms/C. 2118.

WAR DIARY
or
INTELLIGENCE SUMMARY

(Erase heading not required.)

Army Form C. 2118

Instructions regarding War Diaries and Intelligence Summaries are contained in F.S. Regs., Part II. and the Staff Manual respectively. Title Pages will be prepared in manuscript.

Place	Date	Hour	Summary of Events and Information	Remarks and references to Appendices
Trenches	6.viii.17		Enemy artillery activity slight.	Casualties, Wd. O.R. 5
Do	7.viii.17	9.30 PM	Relieved by (112th Bde. 37th Div.) Moved to Camp nr BEAVER CORNER route via WYTSCHAETE & VIERSTRAAT. Bn in Reserve	Bde O.O. No 156 Casualties Wd.r.r. Bdy. Capt FENTON
BEAVER CORNER 28 N.15.c.9.9			Do	
Rd. Map Fr. Sheet 27 STAFFORD CAMP	8.viii.17	4.30 PM	Relieved by (63rd Bde.) Marched to Camp via Mt NOIR. Weather very wet. Arrived camp 7.30 P.M.	
27 R 24.0.5				
Do	9.viii.17		Routine. G.O.C. 57th Bde. Brig. Gen T.A. Cubitt addressed Bn. & complimented them on success of work in the Trenches since June. Transport by road to QUESQUES Area.	Bde O.O. No 157
Do	10.viii.17		Do. Advanced party under Major SHAKESPEARE to QUESQUES area by Train.	B.M. O.O. No 53
Do Ref: Maps HAZ. 5.A. CALAIS.13	11.viii.17	4.25 A.M 9.25 A.M	March to BAILLEUL 11" Train to WIZERNES arrd 11.30 A.M March to QUESQUES. A Coy billeted at VERVAL. H Q QUVELINGHEM. Arrived 5 P.M B.C.D. Quesques.	Do
QUESQUES				
Do	12.viii.17		Routine.	
Do	13.viii.17	12 noon	Inspection of 57th Bde by Genl PLUMER IInd Army Commander at HARLETTES.	
Do	14 – 15 viii.17		Routine. Draft of 84 O.R. arrd 17.viii.17 from Base.	
Do	18th viii.17	11.30 A.M.	Presentation of medal ribbons & address to 57th Bde by Major Genl BRIDGES commdg 19th Divn at BULESCAMPS. Recipients in Bn. Capt J BELL M.C./ 40828 Sgt GREENAWAY J. (A.Coy) M.M./29866 Pte CLIFF A (C.Coy) M.M.	
Do	19.viii.17		Routine. Bde Sports Meeting	
Do	20.viii.17		Do. Divl " "	
Do	21.viii.17		Do. " Ft.tb.t ".	

M.B.

Army Form C. 2118

WAR DIARY
or
INTELLIGENCE SUMMARY
(Erase heading not required.)

Instructions regarding War Diaries and Intelligence Summaries are contained in F. S. Regs., Part II. and the Staff Manual respectively. Title Pages will be prepared in manuscript.

Place	Date	Hour	Summary of Events and Information	Remarks and references to Appendices
QUESQUES BELLEBRUNE	21.viii.17	10.30 AM	March to billets at BELLEBRUNE (3 Coys + HQ) - D Coy to ALINCTHUN.	Bde OO No. 158 Bn " 54
BELLEBRUNE	23.viii.17 24.viii.17		Routine	
Do	25.viii.17		Bn sea bathing at ECAULT (by lorry). Bde Title shooting Comp.n won by 10 Worc. Regt.	
Do	26.viii.17		Transport & billeting party to WALLON CAPPEL	Bde OO No. 159
Do	27.viii.17		Routine.	
LE NIEPPE	28.viii.17	8.30 AM	Bn moved by bus to billets in LE NIEPPE Area. Arrd 4 P.M.	Bde OO No 160 Bn " 55
MOULENACKER	29.viii.17	10 AM	Bn marched to billets at MOULENACKER. Arrd 2 p.m.	Bde OO No 161
Do	30.31 viii.17		Routine.	

Army Form C. 2118

WAR DIARY
or
INTELLIGENCE SUMMARY

(Erase heading not required.)

Instructions regarding War Diaries and Intelligence Summaries are contained in F. S. Regs., Part II. and the Staff Manual respectively. Title Pages will be prepared in manuscript.

Place	Date	Hour	Summary of Events and Information	Remarks and references to Appendices

APPENDIX A. ROLL OF OFFICERS DURING MONTH. AUGUST 1917

	OFFICERS DOING DUTY WITH UNIT			NAME	REMARKS
LIEUT. COLONEL	NAME	REMARKS			
MAJORS	SWORD W.D.	Rejd from Army School 14.viii.17	ADJUTANT	CAPT. SNOOK F.J.	Leave 2.viii.17 - 12.viii.17
	SHAKESPEARE W.	Leave 17.viii.17 - 29.viii.17	Q^R M^R	LIEUT. CREWE F.	
CAPTAINS	GIBSON F.A.S.		TRANSPORT OFFICER	CAPT. BAINBRIDGE A.H.	
	EATON G.M.	G.H.Q visitors H^o 12 - 31.viii.17		OFFICERS ATTACHED	
	COLLS E.J.		LIEUT. COL (Comdg. Officer)	DAKEYNE H.W.	Royal Warwick Reg^t Leave 30.viii.17
Lt a/ CAPT.	MEIR W.H.		CAPT	ARMSTRONG G.W.	R.A.M.C.
2/Lt a/ CAPT	BELL J.		2nd LIEUT (cont^d)	HANCOCK B.S.	To Course 25.viii.17
LIEUTENANTS	BOOTH C.A.S.			BEECH A.H	D^o
	DEANE E.W			PINDER M	J^d 3.viii.17 - To Course 26.viii.17
	CLARKE F.			GOUGH H.F.	To Course 10.viii.17
2nd LIEUT.s	GOOD F.C			GREAVES A.F.W.	From Course [illegible]
	SMETHURST R.J.			SMITH R.P.	J^d 3.viii.17. Killed in action 5.viii.17
	LUCAS C.				
	SHIRLEY C.				
	RANDLE M.G.				
	WHITEHEAD W.F.	from leave			
	BUCKLAND A.				
	COTTERILL R.T.	Leave			
	CARVER G.S.				
	OWEN R.W.				
	JOELS	J^d 31.viii.17			

Army Form C. 2118

WAR DIARY
or
INTELLIGENCE SUMMARY
(Erase heading not required.)

Instructions regarding War Diaries and Intelligence Summaries are contained in F. S. Regs., Part II. and the Staff Manual respectively. Title Pages will be prepared in manuscript.

APPENDIX B

MONTHLY ROLL OF CASUALTIES.

Date	No. Rank & Name	Coy	Date	No. Rank & Name	Coy	Date	No. Rank & Name	Coy	Remarks and references to Appendices
KILLED IN ACTION			**Wounded**						
4.viii.17	34803 L/Cpl. McEWAN	A	4.viii.17	*34910 L.Cpl. REILLY J.	B	6.viii.17	40551 Pte WILKES S.	D	*rejoined wounded duty
5.viii.17	22456 Pte GRATTON E.S.	B		24633 Sgt. REDDISH T.	A		23515 " HODGSON S.	D	
	16425 " EDWARDS J.	"		40452 Pte GARDINER P	A		40782 " HAPSHALL H.S.	C	rejd 9.viii.17
	235125 " WRIGHT H	A		5694 L.Cpl. BASELEY R	B	7.viii.17	CAPT. G.M. EATON		rem'd at duty
	40549 " WALKER J.	"		34666 Pte PATTERSON T.	D	9.viii.17	40686 Pte HITCHIN T.H	C	
	2nd Lieut SMITH R.P		5.viii.17	6750 Sgt AMOS J.T.	D				
				31917 Pte LUNN M.H.	B				
				40712 L.Cpl YANCE W.S.	C				
				34935 Pte TURNBULL W	A				
				29809 " SOLLOM C.	A				
				40749 " HIBBERT H	B				
				40564 " ELLERBY C.	B				
				40639 " BAKER A.	B				
				27449 " WEBB J.	B				
				(rej'd 7.viii.17)					
DIED OF WOUNDS									
1.viii.17	27389 Pte COATES T.	B							
6.viii.17	23515 " NUNN J.	A							
	40495 L/Cpl BROWN G.	"							
10.viii.17	25619 Pte TAYLOR T.	"							

Army Form C. 2118

WAR DIARY
or
INTELLIGENCE SUMMARY
(Erase heading not required.)

AUGUST

Place	Date	Hour	Summary of Events and Information	Remarks and references to Appendices
	21/8/17		APPENDIX C
HONOURS + AWARDS.
Copy of 19th Div. Q.542/6. "The Corps commander after going through his various claims has allotted decorations as follows
8.N STAFF Regt.   1 Grenatier wpr
                  1 Field Gun.

APPENDIX D
STRENGTH on 1st + 31st of Month
            Effective   Ration Strength
         Off.   O.R.   Off.   O.R.
Aug 1.   42   772   23   708
" 31.   41   732   22   566

                                        MBJ. | |

WAR DIARY or INTELLIGENCE SUMMARY

Army Form C. 2118

8th (S) Battn North Stafford Regt

1917

Place	Date	Hour	Summary of Events and Information	Remarks and references to Appendices
R/ Sheet 27 MOOLENACKER	Sept 1		Training under Battn arrangements	
"	2		" "	
"	3		Practice attack scheme by NCO's of Bde	
"	4		Battn attack practice. 250 O.R. to 82 J Coy Bde. g 583	
"	5		Routine training	
SHEET 28 EPSOM CAMP WESTOUTRE	6		Move 9 a.m. to Epsom camp. Take over from 7th K.N.L. arrive 12.10 pm. draft 38 ORs	
Mic b.1.1.	7		Battn attack practice Schools. Draft 130 ORs	
"	8		" "	
"	9		Bde attack scheme	
BOIS CONFLUENT TRENCHES I 30/6	10		Move to Bois Confluent 9 a.m. Relieving 13th R.R.R (37th Div) H. 26 pm	
"	11		Relieved 10th K.N.L 1 Coy FRONT LINE 1Pltn IMAGE CRESCENT 1 Coy Res/1Pltn CATERPILLAR Bde OO 165 Relief Cpt 1.0 am	
"	12		Quiet day. Front line Coy relieved by one from CATERPILLAR 2 Coys SUPPORT 1-3rd	
BOIS CONFLUENT	13		Front line relieved by 8th Gloster Dus support Coy by 10th Warwicks	
KEMMEL SHELTERS	14		Battn moved to BOIS CONFLUENT CAPT G. N EATON 15 hospital moved to KEMMEL SHELTERS Bde OO 166	
"	15		Battn attack practice	
"	16		" "	
"	17		Bde attack scheme	
"	18		Relieved batt. of 13 R.B. in trenches 1 Coy to SIEGE. FM Area Relief Complete by 15 midnight	

Army Form C. 2118.

8 (S) Batt N. Stafford Regt.

WAR DIARY or INTELLIGENCE SUMMARY.

(Erase heading not required.)

Place	Date	Hour	Summary of Events and Information	Remarks and references to Appendices
TRENCHES 1 MILE E of HILL 60	July 19		The Battn moved forward into its assembly position for attack A & C Coys occupied British front line in I.31.a and D Coy occupied trenches at HILL 59 in I.36.b The Battn was commanded by Major W. Shakespeare (later on by Lt Col. Wm Bakeyne D.S.O.) A Coy was commanded by Lt Col A.S. Boots B Coy by Capt W.P. News C Coy by Capt E.J. Biell later on by Lt J.H. Dyough B.S.O D Coy by Capt E.J. Coll later by Lt J. Bearre. Disposition of Companies Direction of advance 118° True	
			C Coy on Right B " in centre A " on left D " in reserve Most of the assembly positions were occupied in good time. 12 platoons of C Coy and 3 platoons of D Coy only reached their positions a few minutes before ZERO The Batt. were taken forward by 3A, 4, 9 Gough B.S.O who was commanding a platoon of C Coy. Our casualties in reaching the assembly positions were slight At ZERO (5.50 am) the first platoon of B Bn Regt moved forward and in the first 9 minutes our THE GREEN LINE (the first objective about ½ mile away) the 3rd had to wait here every 19 strongly and captured the BLUE LINE (the final objective about another ½ mile away). The attack was successful and our casualties were not heavy, most of them were	
	20th			

Army Form C. 2118.

8"(S) Batt A Staff[college]

WAR DIARY
or
INTELLIGENCE SUMMARY.

(Erase heading not required.)

Place	Date	Hour	Summary of Events and Information	Remarks and references to Appendices
TRENCHES	5/8/[1]...		From Shell fire which was heavy especially on the former British front line + RESERVE line from L to R fire from our left.	
		01- ZERO + 35 mins	D Coy (Kearney) moved up as ordered to our former front line. There they to the when they arrived by the Commanding Officer to a position on line with Bn H.Q. B there up had moved forward about 400 YDS E.S.E. from there A.0.13. Platoon were sent forward to reinforce B Coy in the front line – 2 of B of BELGIAN WOOD. The remainder consolidated in 2 of SUPPORT POSTS while we were attacking BELGIAN WOOD. 2 & BARRACKS O Coy with half of his Platoon two Vickers Guns 2 & attachment from the 5th M.G. Coy advanced with the Batt on our left (16th M[anchesters]) with orders to establish a machine gun with a position near NORTH FARM from which he would enfilade our own front. This he did after a short sharp fight in which he captured some 5/Guard and 29 prisoners. It was enfilading our left flank. It Germans had been boys without very much difficulty our consolidated our position fly and at times heavily our artillery hard heavily at times and at 7/6 p.m. heat off a German counter attack which we saw developing on the ridge E. of BELGIAN WOOD. Our aeroplanes were very active a considerable number	SA

Army Form C. 2118.

WAR DIARY Bn M Clafford Log
or
INTELLIGENCE SUMMARY.

8"(S)

(Erase heading not required.)

Instructions regarding War Diaries and Intelligence Summaries are contained in F. S. Regs., Part II. and the Staff Manual respectively. Title pages will be prepared in manuscript.

Place	Date	Hour	Summary of Events and Information	Remarks and references to Appendices
TRENCHES	Sept 20		of the enemy aeroplanes came over our front posts after the attack flying low. One was brought down as our night.	
	27th		Machine gun fire. Our position was further consolidated but heavily shelled during the day. The Batt was relieved at night by 1st/7 Kg Lancs Relief complete 3AM The Casualties were as follows	
			Killed 2Lt H J Gough D.S.O. 51 Other ranks	
			Died of wounds 2/3 A.S.W. Greaves + Other ranks	
			Wounded Capt J N S Gibson Wst Brown 2Lt Wst J Barklam E J Joels R W Owen W S Whitehead A Buckland G S Cawey M C } Remained on duty Capt G W Armstrong (RAMC) 173 Missing 35 ORs	
			Other Ranks	Total Officers 11 ORs 263

Army Form C. 2118.

WAR DIARY
or
INTELLIGENCE SUMMARY.

6(S) Batt. No. Stafford Regt.

(Erase heading not required.)

Instructions regarding War Diaries and Intelligence Summaries are contained in F. S. Regs., Part II. and the Staff Manual respectively. Title pages will be prepared in manuscript.

Place	Date	Hour	Summary of Events and Information	Remarks and references to Appendices
KEMMEL SHELTERS	22.		The Battn. moved back to KEMMEL SHELTERS. Roll Call. General clean up etc. Re-organisation.	
	23		Routine work	
	24		"	
	25		"	
	26		Battn. moved to Bivouacs in BOIS CARRÉ. 2/Lt A Bolland on course	
	27		" SPOIL BANK (Jan Corp)	
	28		"	
	29		Two Coys to go to LARCH WOOD TUNNELS (C+D Coys) two Coys to BOIS CONFLUENT at B. working parties	
	30		Lt B W Frane proceeded on course	

H.S. Dakeyne Lieut.-Col.
Commanding 6th (S) Batt. Stafford Regt.

WAR DIARY or INTELLIGENCE SUMMARY

Army Form C. 2118.

8(5) Batt NORTH STAFFORD Regt

Place	Date 1917	Hour	Summary of Events and Information	Remarks and references to Appendices
LEFT FRONT SECTOR	Oct 1		The Battn relieved the 10th R. Warwick Regt in Left Sector. B.C.D. Coys front line. A Coy support. Capt Snook to I/c Left Sector. O.C. 19th Divisional Wing Camp at O.C. 19th Divisional Wing.	Reinforcements
Trenches	2		Quiet day	
"	3		"	
"	4		Heavy Shelling. British attacks on own left. A Coy (Support Coy) heavily shelled	
"	5		The Battn relieved at night by 7" S. Lancs (66"Bgd) proceeded to CLEM CAMP by lorry from ST. ELOI. 2nd/Lt E.A. Goss joined the Battn reported to A Coy. Total casualties during tour 57. O.R.	
CLEM CAMP N.20.b.65.90	6		Cleaning up and re-organisation. Lt F.C. Good and W.O. R.S. Caul on working party to ZEVECOTEN SIDINGS	
"	7		Cleaning up. Baths at KEMMEL	
"	8		Renfries	
"	9			
"	10		2/Lt R.T. Cotterill (A Coy) to hospital. Bn relieved 9" Welsh Regt in Support (58 Bgd) HQ. A. C. Coys SPOIL BANK. B+D Coys. The BLUFF. Surplus personnel 15 KEMMEL SHELTERS working party from ZEVECOTEN. 2/Lts P.H. MOSS, P.E. STEARN. G.F. WARE. G.V. WOOLLEY. C. GAFFORD. A. STONEMAN joined the Battn.	
SPOIL BANK	11		Surplus personnel working at KEMMEL Bn in outpost providing working parties. Operation orders issued. (re evacuation of ZANDVOORDE RIDGE by the Enemy)	

Army Form C. 2118.

WAR DIARY

8'(S) BATT. or NORTH STAFFORD. REGT.

INTELLIGENCE SUMMARY.

(Erase heading not required.)

Instructions regarding War Diaries and Intelligence Summaries are contained in F. S. Regs., Part II. and the Staff Manual respectively. Title pages will be prepared in manuscript.

Place	Date	Hour	Summary of Events and Information	Remarks and references to Appendices
SPOIL BANK	Oct 12		2/L C Shirley on leave to England. 2/L A E Stears Sub-area Commandant at SPOIL BANK. Surplus personnel routine at KENNEL SHELTERS. The Battn provided working parties 150. OR for carrying purposes	
"	13		working parties. Routine for surplus personnel	
LEFT FRONT SECTOR	14		Surplus personnel rejoins companies at SPOIL BANK. The Battn relieved the 7 E.LANCS & 7 S. LANCS in left sector B C & D Coys in front line A Coy (SUPPORT) in IMAGE RESERVE "CORNER HOUSE". H.Q. at I.25.c.9.3 Capt. E.J. COLLS to hospital	
TRENCHES	15		Holding line. Heavy shelling of back areas 2/L P H MOSS and four OR's gassed while on carrying party	
	16		Holding line 2/L's to B Thorley joins the Battn	
	17		Bn relieved by 10 R. Warwicks Regt proceeded to H.Q. Coy HILL 60. B Coy LARCH WOOD A & D SPOIL BANK during tour in line 3 OR's wounded	
SUPPORT	18		Provided working parties cleaning up Sinwell	
	19		Battn relieved by 9 R Welsh Fusiliers (58 Bde) proceeded to BOIS CONFLUENT	
BOIS CONFLUENT	20		Cleaning up providing working parties B Ledus granted leave to the CHANNEL ISLES. The following awards were published in connection with operations on Sept 20th E of YPRES T/Capt G. W. ARMSTRONG. R.A.M.C. attd 8th Staffords Regt. D.S.O	

Army Form C. 2118.

WAR DIARY
8th (S) BATT or NORTH STAFFORD REGT.
INTELLIGENCE SUMMARY.
(Erase heading not required.)

Instructions regarding War Diaries and Intelligence Summaries are contained in F. S. Regs., Part II. and the Staff Manual respectively. Title pages will be prepared in manuscript.

Place	Date	Hour	Summary of Events and Information	Remarks and references to Appendices
BOIS CONFLUENT	20		2/Lt G.S. CARVER Bar to M.C.	
			T/Capt F.A.S. GIBSON M C	
			2nd Lt -a/Capt F.T SNOOK M C	
			40828 . C.S.M. Greenway G. A Coy ⎫	
			13175 C.S.M Kelly E. D Coy ⎪	
			18437 L/Cpl Dearille C. A Coy ⎬ D.C.M.	
			40482 Sgt Seaney G.W. C Coy ⎪	
			43209 Pte Mooney J. C Coy ⎭	
			34814 Sgt Davidson A. A. Coy ⎫	
			18217 " Taylor J. B " ⎪	
			9043 " Steele G.W. A " ⎪	
			12396 " Brindley A. B " ⎪	
			34904 Pte Micklem J. A " ⎪	
			14125 " Brookes J. attached 57 Bde H.Qrs. ⎬ M.M.	
			40750 " Hopes F. D Coy ⎪	
			28452 " Downton J. B Coy ⎪	
			18246 L/Cpl Facey F. C Coy ⎪	
			40784 Pte Dyke J. D " ⎪	
			8126 " Brownhall D " ⎪	
			40252 " Ryle R. D " ⎭	

(A8001) D. D. & L., London, E.C. W. W1771/M2031 750,000 5/17 **Sch. 52** Forms/C2118/14

Army Form C. 2118.

WAR DIARY
8" (S) BATT or NORTH STAFFORD REGT
INTELLIGENCE SUMMARY.
(Erase heading not required.)

Instructions regarding War Diaries and Intelligence Summaries are contained in F. S. Regs., Part II. and the Staff Manual respectively. Title pages will be prepared in manuscript.

Place	Date	Hour	Summary of Events and Information	Remarks and references to Appendices
BOIS CONFLUENT	21		Improvement of camp. Cleaning up. Providing working parties. 1 O.R killed 4 O.Rs wounded	
	22		Improvement of camp working parties	
	23		" "	
	24		" "	
	25		" "	
	26		" "	
	27		" " Battn. relieved 1/2	
CLEM CAMP	28		7 & 5 LANCS (56 Bde) at CLEM CAMP working parties provided. Casualties O.R. killed 1 wounded 2 Pt. H A G Brown & Lt Rawson joined the Battn	
"	29		Cleaning up. Improvement of camp. Drill Routine	
TOURNAI CAMP	30		Bn. Bn. marched to TOURNAI CAMP. Routine	
"	31		Battn route march. VIERSTRAAT. HALLEBAST CORNER. MILLEKRUISSE CORNER. CLEM CORNER rd. will	

H. S. Barnard .... Lieut.-Col.
Commanding 8th (S) Batt. North Stafford Regt.

WAR DIARY or INTELLIGENCE SUMMARY.

Army Form C. 2118
8 N Staffs

Place	Date 1917	Hour	Summary of Events and Information	Remarks and references to Appendices
TOURNAI CAMP.	1		Battalion route march. Route VIERSTRAAT, KEMMEL, LINDENHOEK, DRANOUTRE, KEMMEL SHELTERS, CLONCORNER.	
VIERSTRAAT	2		Bn. Training routine. 2/Lt. A. Buckland proceeded on Signalling Course to 1 x Corps Signalling School LE LEVRETTE	
"	3		Routine. Divine Service	
"	4		Bn. relieved 7th E. Lancs Regt. in the left sector HOLLEBEKE J/10,010. J.26.6.6.1. – J.32.C.2.5. B's C D Coys front line. 'A' Coy in support. Bn proceeded by bus to St ELOI, march through SPOIL BANK LARCH WOOD. Night Relief. Relief completed in good time.	
Trenches	5		Quiet day nothing to report	
"	6		Some hostile shelling in Suffolk. Generally quiet	
"	7		Bn. relieved by 10 R. Warwick Regt. Relief completed without casualties. Bn. took over from 10 R. Warwicks at HILL 60, SPOIL BANK, LARCH WOOD.	
In Support	8		Carrying parties furnished. Normal	
"	9		"	
MOOLENACKER	10		Bn. moved to MOOLENACKER. Route S.P.9. N Edge of BOIS CARRÉ cross country to VIERSTRAAT – WYSCHAETE. Then by lorry. Companies at disposal of O. Coys for cleaning up.	
"	11		"	
LECROQUET	12		Bn. moved by train and route march to LECROQUET. Bn. marched to CAESTRE where it entrained for EBBLINGHEM. Detrained at EBBLINGHEM. Then marched to billets at LECROQUET. Taken over from 2nd Devons 7th DIVISION. 'A' Coy at Puisseux attached BLARINGHEM. Capt. G. Smith reported from England. Capt. N.D. Slamon joined from Reinforcement Camp.	
"	13		Coys at disposal of O. Coys	
"	14		Routine Bn training. Drill Musketry Bayonet fighting. Elementary.	
"	15		Routine Bn Training. C.O. inspected 'B' Coy at 9am D Coy at 9.45am	
"	16		Routine Bn training. Lt. C.H. Phillips. MR RC USA. 10th neurosurgeon of M.O.	
"	17		" C.O. inspected 'C' Coy at 9am. A Coy at 9.50 am	
"	18		" Divine Service. CO inspected billets	

Army Form C. 2118.

WAR DIARY
or
INTELLIGENCE SUMMARY.
(Erase heading not required.)

Instructions regarding War Diaries and Intelligence Summaries are contained in F. S. Regs., Part II. and the Staff Manual respectively. Title pages will be prepared in manuscript.

Place	Date	Hour	Summary of Events and Information	Remarks and references to Appendices
LE CROQUET	Nov. 19. 1917		Routine Bn training.	
"	20		"	
"	21		Major J.G. Franks MC 10th ran auto gd in command. up on 2.11.17 (10 R. Norwich Regt) Lecture Identification to 15 Officers by Lieut Russell 19th Division I.O. Routine Bn training. "C" & "A" Coy attended Gas demonstration at Divisional Gas School. Capt Hancock returned from leave.	
"	22		Routine Bn training. Lieut Good proceeded on leave.	
"	23		Routine "	
"	24		Divine Service. CO inspected billets. Lecture Brigade H.Q. on Modern Pack Lt.	
"	25		At H.S. Villers. Proceeded to Corps Reinforcement Camp.	
"	26		Routine Bn Training. 2 Lt. C. Shirley proceeded G.H.Q. School LE TOUQUET for an Gun Course.	
"	27		" 80 O.R. "B" Coy attend Gas Demonstration at Divisional School.	
CORMETTE	28		Bn. proceeded to CORMETTE CAMP, TILQUES AREA for practice march. Route ARQUES, ST OMER, ST MARTIN and AERT.	
"	29		Bn fired three practices in range. Light good. Wind strong. Results fair. Details left at LE CROQUET proceeded to new billets at CAMPAGNE. Route BLARINGHEM – WARDRECQUES. Bn. continued firing light how. wind mild. Weather Squally. During afternoon Bn proceeded to new billets in CAMPAGNE WARDRECQUES area. Route ST MARTIN AU LAERT, ST OMER.	
"	30		LE TOUQUET proceeded. CO went to LE TOUQUET for demonstration returning same day.	

H. M. Sokoyne Wealth
Conds 8th R. Stafford Regt

WAR DIARY or INTELLIGENCE SUMMARY

Army Form C. 2118.

8th (S) Battn 1 North Staffordshire Regt.

Place	Date	Hour	Summary of Events and Information	Remarks and references to Appendices
CAMPAGNE ST OMER	Dec. 1		Coys at disposal of OC Coys until 11 a.m. Battn Ceremonial parade at 11.30 am to dispose of unusual Commanders war trophy. Afternoon Recreation.	
	2		Routine Inspection of billets by C.O. Battn played 6 Gloucester Regt at football for Divisional Cup.	
	3		2/Lt Lucas proceeded on leave. Routine. Battn parades. Battn Signallers won Signallers Cup. Battn Officers won Big Drum marching Competition	
	4		Routine. Battn practiced attack scheme. Transport won 1st prize in G.O.C. 57th Bde Transport Competition Generally Congratulated N.C.O's & men tall turnout. Battn played "D" wireless at football. Lost 2.1. ½ NTM & Ram-tall went off leave. 2/Lt N.B. Gore proceeded to 91 Corps Reinforcement Camp as a Musketry instructor	
	5		Routine. Advance party sent forward to new area under Station football match	
	6		The Battn left CAMPAGNE at 2.0 PM marched to 5. OMER & entrained at 5.10 PM Battn minus Transport detrained at MONDICOURT (nr DOULLENS) at 11 PM, D Coy remained at our unloading party, the remainder of the Battn marched to POMMIER (9 miles)	
POMMIER	7		Arrived POMMIER 3.30 am. Battn rested General clean up. Day devoted to	
POMMIER	8		The Battn marched to BAPAUME and detained at LE TRANSLOY at 3.15 PM Battn marched to ETRICOURT via RECQUIGNY LE-MESNIL - MANANCOURT and arrived at TINCH (Camp outside ETRICOURT) at 8.15 PM	

Army Form C. 2118.

WAR DIARY
8th (S) Batt North Staffordshire Regt
INTELLIGENCE SUMMARY.
(Erase heading not required.)

Place	Date	Hour	Summary of Events and Information	Remarks and references to Appendices
ETRICOURT TRENCHES APP. RET	8		The 57th Bde was then in III Corps Reserve	
NINE WOOD 1/10,000	9		The advance party of the Battn went up the line to reconnoitre. The 57th Bde relieved the Res Bn (16th Inf Bde of the 6th Division) 2/8. Battn marched from ETRICOURT via EQUANCOURT - FINS - METZ - TRESCAULT to HINDENBURG LINE. HQ RIDGE TRENCH L.31.d.k0.10 and relieved 8th Bedford Regt. R Davison 2/5 CARVER MC DCM + 1 O.R. wounded. (2/5 CARVER 2C9 remained at duty)	
HINDENBURG LINE	10		The Battn relieved the 2 D.L.I. (18th Inf Bde) in the RIGHT SUB. SECTOR. A Coy R FRONT LINE C. D Coys in SUPPORT B. L FRONT LINE BHQ. L.20 d. c.9 Relief complete at 11.15 PM.	
TRENCHES	11		Quiet day. Great hostile air activity	
"	12		Battn posted to B Coy. G.O.C. 19th Division came round trenches 2/5 FLANNIGAN joined	
"	13		Quiet day. Two platoons C Coy took over part of FRONT LINE between A-B Coys	
"	14		TRENCH ROUTINE. The 57th Bde was relieved by 58th Bde.	
HINDENBURG LINE	15		into the Reserve Bde Area. The Battn was relieved by 7th E. Lancs moved into HINDENBURG LINE took over from 7th S Lancs. A Coy RIDGE SUPPORT. D Coy VALLEY TRENCH B " RIDGE TRENCH C. " VALLEY SUPPORT BHQ RIDGE TRENCH L.31 d.45.10	

Army Form C. 2118.

WAR DIARY or Intelligence Summary.

8(S) Bn North Staffordshire Regt

(Erase heading not required.)

Instructions regarding War Diaries and Intelligence Summaries are contained in F. S. Regs., Part II. and the Staff Manual respectively. Title pages will be prepared in manuscript.

Place	Date	Hour	Summary of Events and Information	Remarks and references to Appendices
HINDENBURG LINE MARTRET PINE WOOD J.11.b.00.	15		2/Lt P.B. Moor and A/Cpl proceeded to V Corps School on General (Trunk) course during run in trench killed. 2/Lt R. Beech & 2/Lt Carver M.C. D.C.M. proceeded on leave to England. Trench Routine. General clean up.	
	16			
	17			
	18		Lt. B. Yates, 10 O.Rs moved to HAVRINCOURT WOOD. The Battn came under the command of the G.O.C. 56 Bde. Capt J. Parvin M.C. Joined the Battn 10.30 & took temporary command of C Coy. Bn H.Qs moved to L31.C.54	
	19		Trench Routine. General cleaning up	
	20		B'n Headqrs proceeded to HAWES CAMP (tents) HAVRINCOURT WOOD Relief complete 5 PM. The Battn was relieved by HAVRINCOURT WOOD Relief	
HAVRINCOURT WOOD	21		very cold weather. General clean up of kits. Boots. Baths. 2/Lt 57 R.G.R. rejoined the 8th Bn in the Right Sub Sector. Battn	
	22		Marched from HAVRINCOURT WOOD via METZ – TRESCAULT – returned to 6 Wilts in support H.Qs L10.d.1.1. A Coy L27.c.29. C. Couillet Avenue L33b. B L26.a.B.8 D L33.b. Relief complete 7.30 pm. 2 O.Rs wounded on TRESCAULT–RIBECOURT Rd on way up. Lt. Col H.W. Bakewell DSO Leave to England. 2/Lt E.W.D. Baul " " " Lt. A.J.C. Galton Transferred to England to Tank Corps	

D. D. & L., London, E.C. (A8024) Wt. W14771/M231 759,000 5/17 Sch. 52 Forms/C2118/14

WAR DIARY or INTELLIGENCE SUMMARY

Army Form C. 2118.

8th Batt. North Staffordshire Regt.

Place	Date	Hour	Summary of Events and Information	Remarks and references to Appendices
MADRET WOOD / to the / TRENCHES	22		2/Lt Flanagan to 57" T.M. Battery. Capt Purves M.C. to 57" Bde.	
	23		Trench Routine. Working parties provided (no ops)	
	24			
	25		(Nivelgis 1918) The Battn relieved the 8" Glosters in the RIGHT SUB SECTOR. G.O.C. 57 Bde (Act G.O.C. 19" Bn.) invited Battn HQ. Bn H Qrs L.33.b. 20.75. R FRONT COY L.34.a.2.6 C Coy L.33.b.8.7 D " L.27.d.3.3 B " L.33.b.6.3 A. SUPPORT	
	26		2/Lt Effness returned from leave. Quiet day. Very heavy snowstorms. 2nd/Lt A Shaw & Proceeded to join 2/Lt G Worsley } 2/6" N Stafford Regt.	
			2/Lt Jarvis proceeded on Lewis Gun Course. Capt & S Dando & } C.J. Hunter joined the Battn. Lt Col Gibson wounded.	
	27		Quiet day. Heavy snowstorms. 2/Lt J.C. Good proceeded to E Coy. School to General Course.	
	28		Quiet day two friendly aeroplanes exceptionally air activity enemy ranging on our trenches.	
	29		Air activity. Night. North shelling of our lines B Coy relieved B Coy & Elkington from Coy.	

WAR DIARY or INTELLIGENCE SUMMARY

Army Form C. 2118.

8th (S) Batt North Staffordshire Regt

Place	Date	Hour	Summary of Events and Information	Remarks and references to Appendices
MAP REF NINEVEH (0-0) 1/10,000	30		At 1.30 am Enemy put down a very heavy barrage on our RIGHT & CENTRE Coys who were very heavily shelled the enemy launched a strong attack on our right with the view to capturing WELSH RIDGE. In this he was unsuccessful although he had some slight success in two places entering the lines of the 63rd NAVAL DIVISION. His barrage lasted about 15 hours again repeated during the morning. Enemy firing was kept up during the whole of the day Our casualties were heavy. 2 Lt A DONARD wounded 2 Lt A LINDSAY " 2 Lt V OSBORN " Sent to Hospital	
	31		B Coy relieved C Coy in R FRONT LINE At 9.30 am Enemy put down smoke heavy barrage on our RIGHT CENTRE Coy of the DIVISION on our RIGHT _____ attacked for the two days. Our casualties Killed 15 Missing 8 Wounded 48. 2 Lt F BLAKE M.C. wounded 2 Lt C Shirley " to 7A The Batt was relieved by the 10 WORCESTERS & proceeded to SUPPORT HQ. 1 Sd & 2 Lt. A Coy of the Batn came unstuck the relief of the 10 Worc ___ Awards published in Orders Gazetted _____ published 22nd Capt Act Bar Aidridge M.C. M.C dated 1.1.18 Lt G.A.Clerke _____ Dec 1917	

Army Form C. 2118.

WAR DIARY
or Nott/Hopsholy
INTELLIGENCE SUMMARY.
(Erase heading not required.)

Place	Date	Hour	Summary of Events and Information	Remarks and references to Appendices
MAP REF NINE WOOD 1/10,000 TRENCHES	31		Honors included in London Gaz 315 dated 7th Dec 1917. Mentioned in Dispatches Lt Col Bakeyne DSO Capt Mew W.A. Capt Bryan R.W.W. Lt Dun & Crewe Lt Brandton H. 2/Lt H.P.Gough (DSO) Killed Sept 20.17. C.S.M Simpson (B Coy) List of Officers actually serving with the Battn. Lt Col Bakeyne DSO. Commanding Officer (leave) Major J.G. Hayton MC. 2nd in Command Capt &P Smith MC a.c A Coy " Bell MC " B " (leave) Lt a. Mew " C " " " Act Beech " D " " " G.M Eaton " E Davies (acting Adjutant) 2/Lt B.S Hancock (acting Adjutant) (leave). Lieut C.W Blair	

Army Form C. 2118.

WAR DIARY
8 (Sha) or th Stafford Regt
INTELLIGENCE SUMMARY.
(Erase heading not required.)

Instructions regarding War Diaries and Intelligence Summaries are contained in F.S. Regs., Part II. and the Staff Manual respectively. Title pages will be prepared in manuscript.

Place	Date	Hour	Summary of Events and Information	Remarks and references to Appendices
	31		Lt Co L Hunter	OC 19 Bys
			Lt E Cocking Tay	Retd from leave
			Lt F C Gregg (course)	Lt a/Capt J J Snook MC 2 cm? Adjutant Rgt
			Lt-Qm T Crewe	" B/Prince MC 52 Bn
			2Lt J Atkins	" Cryan 52 B.O
			2Lt J Laird	Lt Siddon Instructor 12 Corps School
			2Lt C Lucas	Lt Lyne " IX Corps R Camp
			2Lt E Wake	2Lt Nutter 19 Division
			2Lt Lord Morley	
			2Lt Carr MC 2cm (leave)	
			2Lt A Jarvis (course)	
			Capt Act Bainbridge MC 52 Bn T.O	
			Lt G Randall (squadron typist)	
			2Lt Brennan (course)	
			2Lt Clarke MC (wounded Dec 31st)	
			2Lt Gibson 36	
			2Lt Downes 30	
			2Lt Lindsay 30	
			2Lt Hare 15 5A Cadre	
			2Lt Sheldon 10 5A Cadre	
			Lt Chairman B.S.A.M.O	

H S Lobeyne Lushford
Comdg. 8th North Stafford Regt

Army Form C. 2118.

WAR DIARY or INTELLIGENCE SUMMARY.

9th (S) Batt NORTH STAFFORD REGT.

Ref. Map. 57. C. N. E.

(Erase heading not required.)

Place	Date	Hour	Summary of Events and Information	Remarks and references to Appendices
MAP REF. NINE WOOD 1/10,000 Thereled	Jany 1		The Battn was in Support of the Left sector of the Divisional Front. Dispositions:- H.Q. L 26 d 7.1. B Coy KABUL - COUILLET AVENUE C. FORK AVENUE D. Trench in L 26 d. A Coy Attached to 10" Worcesters Regt.	
	2		Trench Routine.	
	3		Trench Routine. The Battn relieved the 10"th Warwick Regt in the centre sub sector of the centre Battn of the Left sector of the Divisional front. Dispositions: A Coy attached to 10" Worcesters Regt. H.Q. L 27 c 6.9. B Coy Left Front CHESTER TRENCH L 27 b rd C Coy COUILLET TRENCH L 27 d D Right Front Coy CHESTER TRENCH L 27 a 5.15. to MARCOING - VILLERS PLOUICH R.Y.	
	4		Trench Routine. A Coy fellows [?] returned from IX Corps School as gone.	
	5		Trench Routine. 2/Lt Norman proceeded to 3rd Army Musketry Course	
	6		Trench Routine. Battn was relieved by the 9" Cheshire Regt (58" Inf Bde) - proceeded to support in HINDENBURG LINE.	

WAR DIARY
8(S) BATT N. STAFFORD REGT
INTELLIGENCE SUMMARY

Army Form C. 2118.

Place	Date	Hour	Summary of Events and Information	Remarks and references to Appendices
NINEWOOD.	6	10.0.a.m	HINDENBURG. LINE. Dieparford N.Q. "L.36.C.5.1. A Coy/relieving 10th Worcester Regt	
			A. VALLEY SUPPORT.	
			B. UNSEEN TRENCH	
			C. VALLEY TRENCH	
			D. UNSEEN SUPPORT	
	7		Trench Routine. The Batt n were relieved by one Coy 5th S. Wales Borderers (Pioneers) and proceeded from TRESCAULT by Light Rly to YPRES marched to VALLULART CAMP arrived 7.30 PM.	
VALLULART CAMP	8		General cleanup. Bathing of the Batt n.	
	9		Routine. Baths. Lt Col. European (from Beyrut) returned from leave	
	10		Routine. Baths proceeded working parties (180). Capt Davis attached to 10th Worcester Regt	
	11		Routine. 01/10% wounded on 01/10% wounded Regt attached to the Baths	
	12		The Battn proceeded by light Rly from YPRES to HAVRINCOURT WOOD (4 miles from TRESCAULT) and marched to trenches the 7th S Lancs (56 Inf Bde) on its left Sector of the Right Bdy of the Divisional front relieving Right group: } in Trenches from L34 d 00.35 A Coy Centre: } to L 34 a 10.00 C. } L 34 a. Left: } D. } B Coy Subport L 34 c 60.35.	

Army Form C. 2118.

8th (S) Batt. WAR DIARY or STAFFORD. REGT.
INTELLIGENCE SUMMARY.
(Erase heading not required.)

Instructions regarding War Diaries and Intelligence Summaries are contained in F. S. Regs, Part II. and the Staff Manual respectively. Title pages will be prepared in manuscript.

Place	Date	Hour	Summary of Events and Information	Remarks and references to Appendices
T.0.0.00. NINE X(40g)	13		Trench Routine	
	14		"	
	15		Lt. E.W. Deane to Field Ambulance. Lt. Jarvis returned from Lewis Gun Course.	
	16		Trench Routine. Lt Coates & Lakeyna D.S.O. proceeded to 56th Flying Squadron BERTANGLES for 4 days Leave Duty	
	17		Trench Routine	
	18		The Battn was relieved by the 8th Gloster Regt moved into Support 15 the Right Sector	
	19		Wood TRENCH	
	20		Trench Routine. The Battn was relieved by the 8th Gloster	
	21st		Regt moved to EASTWOOD CAMP. (HAVRINCOURT WOOD) A & D Coy marched. The B & C Coy proceeded by Light Rly.	
EASTWOOD CAMP	22		Routine	
	23		The D Coy marched to trenches relieved the 10th R.B. Warwicks Regt. in the Centre sub, sector of the right sector	
TRENCHES				

WAR DIARY — 2/(5) Batt. STAFFORD REGT.
INTELLIGENCE SUMMARY

Army Form C. 2118.

Place	Date	Hour	Summary of Events and Information	Remarks and references to Appendices
NINE WOOD	23	10.0.a.m	Disposition A. B. D Coy Front Line C Coy Support.	
	24		Trench Routine to Coclus Dakyns Pte returned from fatigue course.	
	25		"	
	26		2/Lt Do Jones } Joined the Battn. 2/Lt E Press 2/Lt Haynes 2/Lt Channings	
	27		2/Lt Stevenson returned from Gallery Instructors Course. Routine. 2/Lt Bates was relieved by the 10/R Warwicks Regt proceeded by Light Rly to VALLUART CAMP.	
	28		Routine	
	29		Routine. Capt Warner 2/Lt Amos & 2/Lt W B Hurley proceeded on leave to England. 2/Lt Randall proceeded to BOULOGNE on escort duty	
	30		Routine. Working party 2/Lts Press wounded by bomb at ECHELLE at 57 Inf Base School.	

Army Form C. 2118.

WAR DIARY — 6(S) Batt N. Stafford Regt.
or
INTELLIGENCE SUMMARY.
(Erase heading not required.)

Place	Date	Hour	Summary of Events and Information	Remarks and references to Appendices
KINGWOOD CAMP	31/10/00		VALLUHART CAMP. Routine. The Bath proceeded by Lorries to TRESCAULT squached Funnels relieving 15/10/16 through Regt in the Centre Sub Sector of the Regt. Group. Relief Complete 7.30 P.M.	
			List of Officers serving with the Batln	
			Lt Col Hn Sakeyre 2i/c Commanding Officer	
			Major J.G. Martin 2nd in Command	
			Capt. J. Snape M.C. Bch. Adjutant (Leave)	
			Capt. G.R. Smith (O/C B Coy)	
			" J. Bell M.C. (O/C A Coy)	
			" J.A. Merr (Leave)	
			Capt. E.M. Eaton (O/C D Coy)	
			" A.W. Beech (O/C C Coy)	
			A.S. Stanesto (Adjt.)	
			Capt. C.A. Bamburg B.M.S.57 Bde. T.O	
			Lt. Orr J. Crewe	
			Lt. F. Good (Course)	
			Lt. A.J. Gellens (Bde School)	
			2/Lt M.G. Randall Signalling Officer	
			2/Lt A.E. Gore (Leave)	
			2/Lt A. Saird	
			2/Lt W.A. Keane	
			2/Lt P.J. Moss (Leave)	
			2/Lt J. Jaynes	
			2/Lt Cpl Lukes	
			2/Lt E.J. Weeks	
			2/Lt E. Channing (Course)	
			2/Lt J.H. Stevenson	
			2/Lt W.B. Shonley (Leave)	
			2/Lt Beenby (attached from 10/R Warwicks)	
			2/Lt A.Q. Allan (Course)	
			2/Lt G. Currie M.C. Dem.	
			2/Lt Jarvis	
			2/Lt S.O. Jones.	
			Detached	
			Capt. Curnow M.C. 57/Bde	
			Capt. Bance 10/R. Warwick Regt.	
			Lt P.W. Evans 57/Bde	
			2/Lt Rickets 57/Bde	

H. W. Sakeyne Lt. Col.
Comdg 8th Bn North Stafford Regt

www.ingramcontent.com/pod-product-compliance
Lightning Source LLC
Chambersburg PA
CBHW081423160426
43193CB00013B/2179